HR Excellence

Improving Service Quality
and Return on Investment
in Human Resources

HR Excellence

Improving Service Quality and Return on Investment in Human Resources

Scott Weston

Excellence Media
San Francisco, California

HR Excellence
Improving Service Quality and Return
on Investment in Human Resources

Copyright © 2006 by Scott Weston

LCCN: 2006908131

ISBN: 978-0-9786927-0-5

Published by
Excellence Media
San Francisco, California

Requests for information should be addressed to:
Excellence Media
3128 16th Street, PMB 142
San Francisco, CA 94103
www.HRExcellence.net

Printed in the United States of America

This book is dedicated to my parents,
who have always believed in me—
even when sometimes I couldn't.
Their love and support has made me
who and what I am today.

CONTENTS

INTRODUCTION

It is not enough to do your best;
you must know what to do, and then do your best.

(W. Edwards Deming, American statistician, 1900–1993)

"HR MUST BECOME MORE OF A
STRATEGIC PARTNER IN THE ORGANIZATION!"

SOUND FAMILIAR? This edict has been cried out throughout the human resources profession and from within organizations throughout the world. It has sent countless HR professionals scrambling to fulfill this mandate, without clear instructions or a plan of how to do it—simply that they must do it.

This book is written for the HR professionals who have been told to be more strategic and contribute to the organization's bottom line. It will bring clarity to these issues, and establish a path to follow so that HR can, first, understand its current organizational position and then, secondly, implement the processes that will improve and increase its value.

HR Excellence is a thorough framework for all HR professionals to follow. It will be a crash course for some and a refresher for others. It provides information applicable to Senior VPs at multinational corporations, but it is also meant for middle managers and front-line HR professionals, as well as HR generalists at the small to medium organizations who find themselves buried in administrative responsibilities.

1

Management has been chanting "Be more strategic!" for years, if not decades, so what exactly are HR professionals supposed to do? When is there the time to do it? And better yet, how do we do this? What steps must we take? What are the tools we should use?

In test marketing the concept of this book over the past several years and talking with fellow HR practitioners at many different levels, it became apparent that without a clear understanding of what role HR currently plays and what fulfilling a strategic role looks like, it is nearly impossible to create a solution and to answer all of these questions.

There is so much information out there—too much, perhaps. I don't know what level you personally hold in your organization, but I do know that you do not have the time to try and find, and then sift through, even a small part of the information that is available. What I have done in this book is to distill concepts and tools from quality and management sciences into a usable form for HR professionals. Condensing this information into a form specifically focused on HR has not been done up to this point, nor put between two covers—until now.

The Need for HR Excellence

The move toward outsourcing part or all of the human resources function continues to rapidly become the norm in many organizations. Why? Because in some organizations, HR is simply a mess —a mess of inefficiency, bureaucracy, and archaic paper-based processes—and something drastic has to be done. Even in well-run HR departments, HR professionals feel the pressure to continue to improve operations. Do more with less; demonstrate and improve the return on investment that company management is putting into your salary and your department's budget.

The traditional body of knowledge in human resources management covers the vast expanse of recruiting, training, benefits, compliance, employee relations—yet it is normally fairly thin on the "management" part. After learning about compliance issues, employment law, and how to train managers about sexual harassment, where do HR professionals learn about improving their own performance, and more efficiently running the HR function?

Beginning with a discussion of quality and the HR function, *HR Excellence* shows you how to pro-actively identify key areas to facilitate improvement, how to use analytical tools to understand your processes better, and how to use technology to innovate, not just automate.

Rounding out the information, I examine Service Level Management and effective implementation of Service Level Agreements (SLAs), detailing the correlation between the cost of quality in HR and how it relates to both hard and soft-money return on investment. I also add to the discussion about the issues of outsourcing—the why's, the what's, its impact on the HR profession—and offer "Six Keys to Successful HR Outsourcing."

Finally, tying it all together, I will give you ways to make sure your improvements and hard work become permanent—able to demonstrate and sustain bottom-line results—and to instill a culture of excellence within your HR function.

Though no book can realistically fix all of HR's problems, *HR Excellence* will help move you forward to that end!

THE INCREASING COMPLEXITY OF THE HUMAN RESOURCES FUNCTION

In today's businesses, the role of HR continues to grow more and more complicated as employment laws and compliance issues become more painfully intricate. Plus, the increased focus on human capital management strategy forces more organizations to look to HR for answers. Of course, the administrative role is still expected, but this is ancillary to the more mission-critical duties that make the modern HR practitioner an employment law expert—in addition to being a key contributor in recruiting, training, and retaining the people who make up the organization.

Increasingly, improving HR quality has been thrust in the lap of HR professionals, along with the push for a more strategic role—

"Fix everything!"

"Measure and improve your processes and overall quality!"

"Provide strategic value and return on investment!"

Add this to a list of ever-mounting responsibilities that stem from current issues of compliance, security, and other factors, and the HR professional's job doesn't just seem overwhelming—it is overwhelming!

The good news is that quality, strategy, and return on investment (ROI) are all connected and can be addressed in tandem by taking a careful look at the operational side of the human resources function, by making adjustments, and by putting controls in place to maintain improvements.

The Knowledge Gap in HR

When it comes to improving operations in the human resources department, many of the disciplines needed to accomplish improvements are often not present in HR. For example, creating a formal process to source for a vendor and following the steps in a Request for Proposal (RFP) is probably second nature to someone in the purchasing department, but it may be a new experience for many in HR. Other "unfamiliar" examples might include:

- Project Management
- Process Mapping
- Statistical Analysis
- Causal Analysis
- Outsourcing
- Financial and Return on Investment Analysis.

ARE YOU READY FOR THE FUTURE OF HR?

The human resources profession has evolved rapidly over
10 to 20 years. The challenge of the HR professional has become
cosmic in scope, and the depth and breadth
of responsibilities have grown exponentially.
The analytical, project management, and
bottom-line oriented skill sets needed for
the role that the HR professional will fulfill
in the future are often not present.

Like a rapid change in any business environment, HR professionals must continue to adapt or perish.

If you are unclear about the areas in which you need the most
development, think carefully about this issue as you go through
the different parts of this book. Identify those areas where you
most need growth and exposure, and map out a plan for your
own professional development.

There Is No Need to Reinvent the Wheel

A great deal of information is already available and you simply
need to look to other business functions and professional disciplines
for the experience and know-how to improve HR operations. The
information technology department (IT), for example, is probably
several years ahead of HR in terms of experience in successfully utilizing outsourcing. Whether or not you have access to IT employees
internally, who might be able to guide you, you can look to the IT profession for information about improving your own HR operations.

Project management is another area with its own body of knowledge and a wealth of information that you can utilize. HR professionals
can look to project management as a source of knowledge on how
to manage complex activities and tasks such as implementing new
HR technology, completing an annual benefits open enrollment, or
managing a special staffing initiative.

The field of quality has a vast amount of tools and information that have already been demonstrated to be effective and usable across other fields and industries. Despite what some people believe, quality is not exclusively germane to manufacturing operations. Many of its tools have been adapted for use in other service-oriented parts of the organization.

Although this information has been available for some time, the problem is that there is *a lot* of information—too much perhaps. The question looms: Where to begin?

At first glance, quality is a discipline that has a seemingly endless amount of terms, acronyms, formulas, tools, and methods that may seem completely incompatible with HR operations. However, there are many valuable elements that can be of benefit to HR.

I am not an engineer and I do not come from a manufacturing background, so many aspects of the quality field were as foreign to me as they may be at first to you. As time went on, I was relieved to find out that I would not have to learn the very technical engineering concepts. Instead, the challenge became discovering what to focus on, and what to ignore.

This book is a quick-start guide to quality, and my goal is to distill this information into something you can quickly grasp and immediately put to use in HR. If you find that you like this taste of quality tools and methods, there is a vast amount of additional information available to you that goes well beyond the scope of this book.

Before HR Has a Full Seat at the Table

If HR truly wants a seat at the executive table and wants to be a strategic contributor, it must first deliver on the operational side of its part of the business. It must be able to validate how HR contributes to the bottom line, and it must be able to prove that it is not just a cost center.

Many organizations believe that outsourcing the transactional and administrative parts of HR is a solution that will allow the human resources staff to focus more on strategic issues. While there are great merits in the pursuit of outsourcing, key success factors of a strategic outsourcing initiative in HR are often lacking (outsourcing will be covered in chapter 11). At a more basic level though, if HR is to effectively utilize outsourcing as a tool to improve operations, it must first understand its own needs and those of its customers.

Whether outsourcing the transactional aspects is a solution or not, HR must still demonstrate that it can deliver efficient and effective daily HR operations. This is not accomplished through a single initiative, but is the result of an ongoing commitment to HR *excellence* that manifests in continuing efforts to constantly improve —and to maintain and build on these improvements over time.

THE FRUSTRATION WITH HR

The public relations image of HR varies from organization to organization, and even within organizations. No matter how competent and effective you are, there are probably lingering memories of bad or ineffective HR people from the past in the minds of executives, managers, and employees at your organization.

If you have not read "Why We Hate HR," the August 2005 article in *Fast Company Magazine*, you need to. The author, Keith H. Hammonds, takes a critical view of HR and addresses the long-standing issue about the need for HR to become a strategic partner, and why this has failed to materialize. His assessment may or may not apply to you or your particular situation, but he gives a voice to the frustrations with HR that exist today, and offers an important perspective for all HR professionals who are focused on improving their area of the business.

 A link to the "Why We Hate HR" article is available in the Online Resource Center (described in the next section, "How to Use This Book.")

How to Use This Book

This book is organized into sections that will guide you through the different areas you will need to understand before starting to implement solutions, and, subsequently, what you will need to do to maintain success on an ongoing basis.

Some of the key things to note are:

- The Structure of the Key Sections
- Approaching HR excellence as a Project
- The Online Resource Center
- Other Icons Used throughout the Book.

The Structure of the Key Sections

As I borrow from different quality teachings, I will be adapting the basic structure of the Six Sigma approach to a *project* and using it *as a broad template for discussing HR process improvement as a whole.* The approach is called DMAIC (pronounced Di-MAY-ick) and this stands for:

Define   Identify your processes, customers, and potential areas for improvement.

Measure Clarify the boundaries of your processes, and gather relevant data.

Analyze Make sense of the data; figure out what it tells you.

Improve Create solutions based on your analysis.

Control Gauge your success, and put controls in place to maintain improvements in the future.

Each section will include a group of chapters that deal with the key issues related to improving service quality and return on investment in HR, and each will be viewed through the DMAIC lens.

Six Sigma: Simply a Management Fad?

Six Sigma is a process-improvement methodology that was created by Motorola in the mid-1980s and made famous through its successful use by companies like General Electric in the mid- to late '90s. Six Sigma is a structured methodology that utilizes statistical analysis to improve processes.

After companies like General Electric reported improvement success from implementing Six Sigma, many organizations raced to adopt it. However, companies that embraced Six Sigma lagged in applying it to the HR function. I believe many HR professionals believe that Six Sigma was merely a fad and that it has simply faded from the spotlight as just another management concept *du jour* that has come and gone.

Six Sigma was more than that, though. It is still very much in use. There are many aspects to it that can be drawn upon to improve HR operations despite the fact that, in the past, the steep learning curve and heavy use of statistics put off most HR professionals.

To clarify, this is not a Six Sigma book.

Although I have researched, written, and spoken at great length about Six Sigma and how it can be applied in HR, I do not believe it is a panacea to HR problems. Confucius said, "Do not use a cannon to kill a mosquito." Six Sigma amounts to just that in many situations because of the:

- Size of the HR department
- Size of the issue being addressed, and
- Resources available.

However, the DMAIC model is basic enough to be adapted quickly and effectively in HR. Thus, my use of these concepts in the book.

If you are interested in learning more about Six Sigma and how it can be applied in HR, please see the Online Resource Center for a white paper on this topic.

Approaching HR Excellence as a Project

If you view the pursuit of HR excellence as a global project in HR, you will be able to take the same divide-and-conquer strategy that many process-improvement methods utilize. From this vantage point, many smaller projects will be spawned from the more global approach. Some of these will utilize the DMAIC process and others may use different methods. As noted, I will be using DMAIC merely as a rough guide.

While this book uses the DMAIC approach in looking at HR excellence as a global project in HR, it is also important to note that a project normally has a set beginning and end, and this is not the case with the pursuit of excellence, which is an *ongoing* activity. The tools that you apply to an individual improvement project will become the tools you can use as part of your ongoing operations—as a uniform way to better manage your processes and to optimize and improve them.

Using the DMAIC structure will allow you to more readily identify the areas which need work, and it will assist you in systematically addressing the necessary improvements or changes to these areas. DMAIC is the structure you will return to again and again when beginning to work on each next issue. Over time, you will drive the inefficiencies and customer issues out of your processes. Some of these improvements will stick and others will need to be revisited. As you improve some things, new issues will arise that need addressing. This is the dynamic nature of business, and the pursuit of excellence is a constant movement in the direction of improvement. *It should be thought of as an ongoing journey and not a destination.*

I would add to that the importance of taking action, and the benefits of the resulting momentum that is gained. Not being a Six Sigma Black Belt*, or, not having the entire HR team trained first

---

* A term given to a trained project manager who has mastered the Six Sigma toolset and has demonstrated experience in running Six Sigma projects.

in a process-improvement methodology or its related tools, are not good excuses for delaying action. Although I'm not condoning reckless process improvement, I really like the following quote that sums up what I mean by taking action *now*:

> *A good plan, violently executed now,*
> *is better than a perfect plan next week.*
>
> (George S. Patton, US General, 1885–1945)

THE ONLINE RESOURCE CENTER

Various tools that are discussed in *HR Excellence* are available in electronic form for readers who would like to utilize them. Items in the resource center are marked with the icon shown here.

This is also a place where you can go in the future to look for resources related to areas covered in *HR Excellence,* such as supplemental reading, a marketplace for access to vendors, and additional training to help you in your journey toward excellence.

To utilize the resource center you will need to register at:

www.HRExcellence.net/resource

Registration is FREE.

When prompted, enter the following purchaser's code:

HRE4675

KEY THOUGHTS AND KEY CONCEPTS—Certain concepts are noted with the key icon. These may be part of a list of key ideas, or individual items worthy of extra note to the reader.

QUICK TIPS—These are tools and tactics that you may be able to implement immediately, or with a minimal learning curve.

Large Organization

Small Organization

SCALABILITY—The concepts in this book have been laid out to be scalable to any size organization. While certain large organizations may already have more robust quality-improvement methodologies in place, such as Six Sigma, I have distilled discussions with hundreds of HR and quality professionals who were using a variety of methodologies and approaches, and I have brought together the key tools and concepts that have had the most success in improving HR operations.

As a result, the ideas and tools contained in this book can be utilized by a cross-functional team to improve HR service at a large, multinational corporation—or it can be used by the sole HR person at a very small organization.

When information is primarily relevant only to a large organization or to a small one, I will mark these sections with the icons at left, to allow readers from those groups to more efficiently find information specific to their needs.

AUTHOR'S THOUGHTS—These represent personal experiences, professional opinions, or may also simply pose alternative positions to challenge current human resources thinking on certain issues.

EXCELLENCE

Effective HR strategy relies on a successful joining of *quality* and *excellence*.

Understanding how to combine qualitative and quantitative measurements to uncover cause-and-effect relationships is the first step.

QUALITY OF SERVICE

STRATEGIC VS. TACTICAL

AREAS TO FACILITATE IMPROVEMENT

REDUCING WASTE

CONTROLLING VARIATION

PERFORMING CAUSAL ANALYSIS

Excellence in HR

We are what we repeatedly do.
Excellence then, is not an act, but a habit.

(Aristotle)

Quality vs. Excellence

W HAT is basic *quality*? This really depends upon whom you ask, because *quality* is a very subjective term. A broad definition of quality in a business context could be: *Meeting customer requirements.*

There are also many definitions of excellence, but the key criterion here is *to excel.*

So, in essence, the juncture of quality and excellence is about excelling, *exceeding* customer requirements, not just *meeting* them.

Therefore, we as HR professionals cannot have excellence or quality in our HR service if we do not understand our customers' requirements. It is that simple. Sadly, though, many organizations try to meet customer requirements without taking sufficient time to listen carefully to the voice of the customer. This is one of the most crucial steps in the move toward excellence in the human resources department.

In discussing this in depth, I will draw on many concepts and tools from the field of quality that have been developed and utilized over the years in the manufacturing realm and, subsequently, in the services arena. We only need to adapt many of these tools for our use in the human resources profession.

Quality and the HR Function

Quality is a term that is not frequently used in the everyday language of HR professionals when speaking about their business function. It is normally reserved for manufacturing and other areas. HR has had an image of being less of a hard-line business function and more of a hands-on *administrative* function. This is because it has lent itself to more readily being measured by quantitative rather than qualitative standards. Many of the performance metrics utilized in HR are quantitative, such as:

- Cost-per-hire
- Number of employees trained
- Number of successful enrollments.

While there has often been at least some measure of customer satisfaction—employee opinion surveys, a complaint box, etc.—the measure of the qualitative aspect of the HR function and its impact on the bottom line has been subordinate to the hard-dollar, hard-number measurements.

Why? One of the biggest reasons is that *quantitative information is easier to gather and prove.*

The key question to ask is *whether the use of qualitative information will be more valuable, or not, in evaluating a particular area of HR.*

What about:

- Cost of a *bad* hire to the organization?
- ROI of training to the organization?
- The number of benefits enrollment packets that were rejected, and the associated costs of correcting and resubmitting them?

Each of these issues can exceed the quantitative costs of recruiting and training if the more global, strategic qualitative impact to the organization is considered.

This is not to say that the prevalent metrics that are quantitatively based should be abandoned, because these numbers are still valuable. The next step must be taken, though, and the more difficult, qualitative aspects of HR must be focused on and measured in order to improve quality. This step toward qualitative measurement offers a huge potential return on investment for your organization.

Quality of Service

Addressing the issue of quality of service in the human resources function is difficult from the perspective of identifying needs. The main problem is simply understanding what HR's *customers*—both internal and external—want, and then providing them with it. What does senior management want? What do line-managers want? What do front-line employees want? Though this sounds simplistic, it does take planning and action to identify how HR can become more of a strategic partner in each instance.

But why hasn't HR already risen to that place of being a *strategic* partner?

One reason is that HR often doesn't completely understand what their customers really want, although they assume they know what their employees want, they believe they know what their line-managers expect of them, and they think they have a clear understanding of the expectations of senior management.

Those who have taken the time to ask only a few internal customers may miss the opportunity to improve departmental quality by generalizing too quickly: believing that the answer of one or more line-managers is the answer for all.

Now, that is not to say that HR practitioners don't try to understand their customers. I am speaking about an issue of degree, and the only way to get better at serving your customers is to spend more time getting to understand their needs. This is also a dynamic relationship that changes over time—as customer priorities shift to those areas of highest concern at the moment. That is to say that the #1 priority this month, if addressed, will no longer remain the #1 priority next month because it is no longer an issue of contention or pain. The needs *were* addressed, per the customer's priorities, but, shortly thereafter, the customer is displeased again and HR wonders why.

What are the results? Frustration emanates on both sides.

HR may feel that the customer:

- Is fickle

- Can't be pleased

- Doesn't know what he or she wants.

The customer may feel that HR:

- Doesn't understand the dynamic business environment

- Is slow and bureaucratic

- Is unable to function at a peer level of support.

These are the echoes of HR's frustrations that reflect the constant shifting of customer priorities.

So can customers ever be satisfied if their attention moves constantly to whatever is next on a long list? Absolutely! The trick is to be one step ahead of serving their needs, and to also create an environment that fosters and elicits constant and never-ending improvement. *Customers don't expect perfection, but they do expect attention.* If your customers know that you are constantly paying attention to their needs, and also improving over time, they will often give you the slack to do just that.

Understanding what the customer wants and prioritizing those wants is as simple as asking. But this is a process that must be accomplished in a methodical manner. I will cover this later in chapter 3 as I talk about the Voice of the Customer (VOC).

Staying one step ahead of a customer's needs sounds difficult to accomplish. As you look at the continuum of customers and suppliers, you also need to look to the *customers of your customers* and gain an understanding of what is expected up the line. If you know what your customer's manager or external customers require of them, it can help you understand how that need travels down the line to where you come into the picture.

QUALITATIVE VS. QUANTITATIVE

Today there exists so much confusion and misuse around the words *quality* and *qualitative* that it is important to take a moment to provide standard definitions of these terms.

It is commonly said of HR professionals that we must:

"Measure the qualitative side of HR," or

"Measure the quality of hires," or

"Mix quantitative with qualitative metrics to gauge HR's performance."

All three of these uses have different meanings.

"Measure the qualitative side of HR"—this is an indication of the level of service, rather than simply the number of transactions.

"Measure the quality of hires"—this is an indication of new hires meeting customer requirements and performing as expected on the job.

"Mix quantitative with qualitative metrics to gauge HR's performance"—this is probably the most misused and misunderstood usage of these terms. Qualitative measures can often be gathered as quantitative measures. For example, 1–5 rating scales of satisfaction from line-managers on a survey (quantitative) helps us to understand the level of service received and whether there was satisfaction or not with the service (qualitative).

What might be missing when turning the measurement of attitudes into qualitative measures is *context*. This may be the information that outlines the measurements and gives them more meaning—for example, expanding a 1–5 scale of attitudes with transcribed comments by hiring managers about an HR service they received. This is the type of information that might help your HR department improve poor scores by understanding why they were given, or to maintain high scores by understanding what helped HR to earn them. *This is an example of an effective mixture of qualitative and quantitative measures.*

Strategy vs. Tactics

Earlier I spoke about the mandate for HR to be more strategic. What exactly does it mean to "be more strategic?" What is the difference between being strategic and being tactical? These two terms—*strategy* and *tactics*—are often misunderstood, used interchangeably, or otherwise confused.

Strategy and *tactics* are military terms that have been adopted as important business concepts. Unfortunately, many people in the business community apply one and think it's the other.

Strategic vs. Tactical:

- Always relative to one another
- Tactics are the set of actions taken to *fulfill* a strategy.

The major strategic goals of HR are not obscure or overly complex. Some examples:

- Align with and serve the goals of the business
- Meet the internal and external customer requirements
- Demonstrate good return on investment and efficiency in operations.

In the chapters that follow, I will be providing tools and approaches that can be used as tactics to achieve overall strategic goals such as those above, as well as to achieve individual strategic goals tailored to your specific needs. By looking first at HR operations, and improving in this area, you will gain experience and develop skills that can be applied elsewhere.

Strategy without tactics is the slowest route to victory.
Tactics without strategy is the noise before defeat.
(Sun Tzu, Chinese General, circa 500 BC)

KEY AREAS TO FACILITATE IMPROVEMENT OF SERVICE

Achieving quality in your operations is easier said than done. If you are striving for excellence as well, it is even more difficult.

To accomplish both quality and excellence—to go beyond just meeting customer requirements—you must focus on the things that keep you *from* meeting customer requirements. To this end, there are three primary areas to think about in an effort to improve HR operations: 1) reduce waste, 2) control process variation, 3) identify the root causes that negatively impact the performance of your processes.

By systematically attacking these, the forces working against your improvements will be cleared away.

Reducing Waste

It is difficult to be strategic when precious resources end up going to waste. Utilizing time and money in a way that is less than optimal will undermine a budget and the return on investment of a human resources department.

Since in HR there are no bad units that get piled up on an assembly line like in manufacturing, waste is something that needs to be more carefully identified. Where do things have to be done over? Where is more time being utilized than necessary? A department that appears busy may seem to be functioning efficiently, and the inherent waste may not be immediately evident.

So how do you go about establishing and finding where waste exists in your processes?

The answer is to carefully understand what it is you do and to actively track "defects" or disconnects with customer expectations. This waste may exist intangibly as time—wasted labor or increased time to accomplish a task. Or, it may manifest within tangible costs (unnecessary vendor fees, regulatory penalties, etc.). I will talk more about the hard- and soft-dollar costs in chapter 15.

Controlling Variation

Variation is the enemy.
(Jack Welch, Past-CEO, General Electric Corporation)

In managing a business process, waste and variation are the enemies. Eliminating waste seems pretty obvious, but many HR professionals do not initially understand how variation in a process is also detrimental.

There is an inaccurate notion that lowering time and costs is always better. This is not necessarily always true. Just as meeting customer requirements translates into quality, eliminating variation translates into business process management. Faster is not necessarily better—nor is being cheaper—if it does not fulfill a customer's requirements.

The root of one of the biggest complaints of customers is in variation; their expectations were not met. This begs the question, "How did they come to that expectation?" Was it agreed upon in advance? Did they just make an assumption?

There is a need to properly align a customer's expectations with what can be delivered in advance, but the next step is to narrow the variation to hit that expectation.

For example, would a moving company showing up three days early be in any way helpful to most people being relocated? In fact, it might evoke as much (or more) upset as a moving company showing up three days late!

Many processes in human resources are filled with variation. A great deal of this happens because of the many variables that are outside the control of HR. Sadly, knowing that *some* of these variables are outside HR's control often translates into a lack of effort to control those variables that HR *does* have control over.

While complete control is probably not achievable, improving control is the goal here. This can be achieved by systematically identifying the variables that impact a process and cause variation in it.

Let's look at an example of *Days to Fill* an open position:

We have a wide bell curve (Figure 1-1) representing days to fill that spans from 5 days to 185 days. That's a big gap. The clustering in the center of the bell curve is between 50 and 90 days, so from open requisition to start date, it is taking around two to three months. This graph prompts some questions:

> Who took 185 days? Why?
>
> Who got hired and was on board in only 5 days?
>
> How was this accomplished so quickly?
>
> Were policies circumvented, such as background screening?
>
> What *aren't* we seeing represented in this chart?
>
> What is the number of candidates that withdrew from candidacy because they had already been hired by another company?
>
> How many withdrew because they were just irritated with the protracted process and felt slighted or strung-along?
>
> Which candidates are still with the company?

Days to Fill

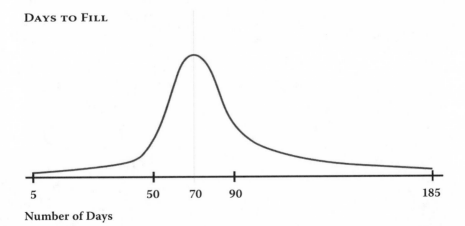

Number of Days

Figure 1-1

Sources of Variation can be:
- Identified
- Quantified
- Mitigated, controlled, or prevented.

Causal Analysis: Identifying the *Right* Problems to Fix

As you identify waste and variation in your processes, there may be an initial urge to install a quick-fix to the problem. To effectively improve your processes, you need to focus on the right things—those things that directly affect your processes. Consider this basic tenet that physicians follow:

Diagnose before you prescribe.

Unfortunately, at the root of many lackluster business-improvement initiatives is a failure to follow this basic rule. And even more importantly you should:

Accurately diagnose before you prescribe.

To do so, you need to carefully look at the key inputs to a process to understand how they influence the outcome or outputs of that process. This is the critical, but sometimes elusive, *cause-and-effect* relationship that tells us what inputs and variables drive outputs and outcomes (both positively and negatively). In other words: *What levers must be pulled to drive HR operations?* Understanding these relationships is the key to improving your operations and driving future performance. In chapter 2, I will identify the key inputs and outputs of your processes, and later, in chapter 8, I will explore tools to understand the cause-and-effect relationship of variables in your processes and how these drive process performance.

Where There's Smoke, There's Usually Fire

In trying to understand the relationship between the key input factors and how a process turns out, anecdotal evidence can play a helpful but not necessarily definitive role in identifying possible areas to fix. You may establish some theories to explore, and some of these hypotheses may be proved correct, but some may not. Complex issues usually have complex solutions. Retention is a good example, where a single factor is rarely tied cleanly to an outcome (e.g., increasing salaries alone will not universally improve retention rates).

It is important to give proper attention to your analysis and not to attempt to engineer conclusions to support a hypothesis. This means gathering data as objectively as possible and making an effort to separate out variables that might be skewing your results.

THE MAIDEN AND THE VOLCANO

Post hoc ergo propter hoc. That is Latin for "after this, therefore because of this." This is called a logical fallacy, otherwise known as a coincidental correlation. A classic example of this type of flawed reasoning is:

> "We threw the maiden into the volcano and it *didn't* erupt; therefore, the fire gods were appeased."

As silly as this example might seem, this type of flawed reasoning happens in business all the time—from decisions being made without understanding the true relationship between actions and outcomes—or process inputs and outputs.

How about this one instead:

> "We gave Bob a big bonus package and he didn't quit; therefore, our compensation package was successful."

Maybe Bob's wife is pregnant and he doesn't want to change jobs until after things settle down. The bonus was appreciated and it sure will help with maternity costs, but Bob wasn't going to risk changing jobs and insurance plans with pregnancy being a pre-existing condition.

The point here is to encourage you to *think* about and *search* for the *real* cause-and-effect relationships.

 **KEY THOUGHT**

The Cost of Poor Quality: Two Choices. Pick One.

Quality is not going to just *happen* in your HR processes.

Basically, you have two choices when it comes to the cost of quality:

    1. You can invest in improving quality

or

    2. Pay for the cost of bad quality.

DEFINE

As you look at HR from a strategic view, it is often difficult to know where to begin on your path to quality and excellence.

The beginning starts with definition: Defining your processes, your customers, and what your customers want. From this, you can identify major areas for improvement and begin to prioritize them into project ideas.

DEFINE PROCESSES AND CUSTOMERS

UNDERSTAND CUSTOMERS AND WHAT THEY WANT

IDENTIFY INITIAL PROJECTS FOR IMPROVEMENT AND CREATE A PROJECT CHARTER

Define 〉Measure〉Analyze〉Improve〉Control

DEFINING PROCESSES
AND CUSTOMERS

If you can't describe what you are doing as a process,
you don't know what you're doing.

(W. Edwards Deming, American statistician, 1900–1993)

T HE HR department is comprised of an assembly of a bunch of different processes (recruiting, training, compensation planning, benefits administration, etc.). Each of these processes can be broken down into more detail, but, at a high level, there are certain aspects of the process that can be identified to help you conceptualize it and manage it better.

Start with the Big Picture

In order to understand your processes, it is important to take a step back and understand the basic parts of each process. Later, in chapter 5, I will look more carefully at these processes and endeavor to map these out to help you gain an understanding of the specific steps and tasks that make up each process. Before I do that, though, it is important to look at the macro level, or the big picture, and to get an understanding of the key elements and phases of a process.

There is a graphical tool that can help you understand the key elements and phases of a process and it is called SIPOC (pronounced Sigh-Pock). SIPOC stands for *Supplier, Input, Process, Output, and Customer.* I will look at making more detailed process maps in chapter 5, but for right now I will define them broadly.

Don't skip this part! Taking the time to define your processes and define your customers may seem rudimentary and you may be tempted to skip this part. Don't! **A clear SIPOC exercise can be invaluable as you move forward. It will help you define and understand the flow of inputs and outputs of a process.** I

WARNING!

will also reference the SIPOC exercise as we move forward and talk about your customers, the process of outsourcing, and other areas. **Even if you have never seen a SIPOC before, it is worth the effort to complete!**

Suppliers   After you have identified the process and the key phases, you need to identify the people involved in the process.

Inputs   The next step is to identify the items involved that are required for the process. These can be physical, such as forms, or it can be information.

Process   A process is a recurring set of activities, events, steps, or tasks that result in a desired outcome.

Outputs   What comes as a result of the process are the outputs. Like inputs, these can be physical, such as *completed* forms, or other information.

Customers   Understanding who benefits from a process is important. The customers of a process may or may not receive the outputs of a process.

For example: An employee is both a supplier and a customer when making a benefit request. The employee may fill out a form (input) and the completed form is an output. But although the employee is also a customer of the process (receiving the requested benefit), and the completed form is an output of the process, the employee does not receive the form as an output. The benefits provider would be one of the other customers receiving the completed form as an output.

A SIPOC Diagram

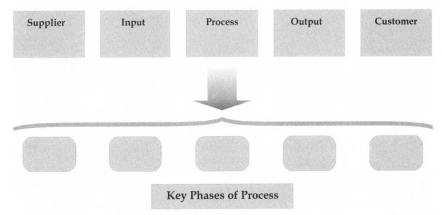

FIGURE 2-1

The Benefits of a SIPOC are:

- Defines boundaries of the process
- Describes where to collect data
- Identifies suppliers and customers
- Identifies inputs and outputs
- Helps support and develop process thinking.

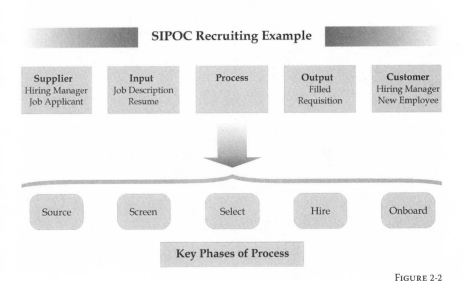

FIGURE 2-2

Processes and Sub-Processes

As you look at a general process, you can readily see the main parts or phases of that process. If you were to drill down beneath each of those phases, there are probably sub-processes with phases that may continue to have sub-processes beneath each of those (Figure 2-3).

The identification and mapping of these different levels of detail depend on what level you are operating to improve or study this process. A thorough streamlining of a process may require granular study of each step and exploration of every sub-process—while an overview of a process as a prelude to outsourcing might make digging too deep into the details of a process a wasted effort, since it will be mostly outsourced.

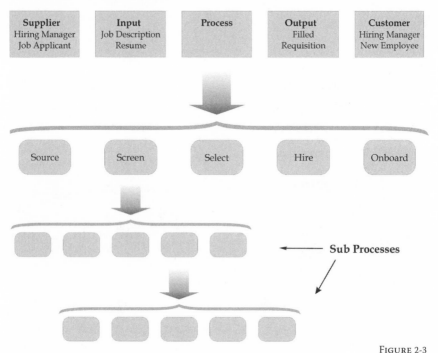

FIGURE 2-3

How to Create a SIPOC Diagram

The SIPOC diagram is illustrated from left to right to demonstrate the transactional flow of supplier to customer, but it is not created as a literal working diagram from left to right. **Please note that the steps are numbered to coincide with the diagram below, which demonstrates the order the** SIPOC **diagram is *created* in— though it is ultimately meant to show the flow from left to right.**

The SIPOC diagram can be completed by following these steps (corresponding to numbers in Figure 2-4).

①	Identify the process.	What does it do?
②	Identify the 4–5 key steps in the process and what the process scope is.	What key things take place in the process? Where does the process start and stop?
③	Identify the outputs of the process.	What comes out of the process?
④	Identify who receives those outputs.	Who are the customers?
⑤	Identify what key inputs the process needs to create those outputs and to function properly.	What is needed for the process?
⑥	Identify who will provide those inputs.	Who supplies what is needed for the process?

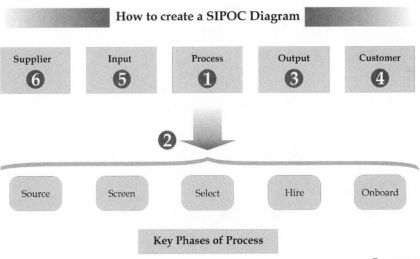

How to create a SIPOC Diagram

| Supplier ⑥ | Input ⑤ | Process ① | Output ③ | Customer ④ |

②

| Source | Screen | Select | Hire | Onboard |

Key Phases of Process

FIGURE 2-4

KEY THOUGHT

The SIPOC exercise is an important tool that will help you understand a process before you begin to try to improve it. It answers key questions and helps you understand:

- Suppliers: Who provides the inputs to the process

- Inputs: The inputs that are necessary to a process

- Process: The activities, events, steps, or tasks that take place in the process

- Outputs: What the process delivers in terms of physical elements, such as information or results

- Customers: Who the process serves.

  SIPOC templates in PDF, MS Word®, and PowerPoint® are available in the Online Resource Center.

Who Are HR's Customers and What Do They Want?

"Excellence" will always be defined by the customer and measured through the perception of how well you meet and exceed customer requirements and expectations.

According to W. Edwards Deming, a statistician and management-science thought leader, you need to understand the following questions:

- Who receives the services that you produce?

- How do they use your service?

- What would happen if you didn't show up today?

- What would happen if you didn't do your job right?

- How do your errors affect them?

- How do find out if you're not meeting the needs or requirements of your customer?

- How far beyond your immediate customers can you trace the effects of what you do?

I have seen a fair amount of resistance from service-oriented professionals regarding the difficulty in gathering information from their processes. It is believed that manufacturing is a much easier system from which to gather data. For example, you can measure the size of a tire as it comes off the assembly line, how many were put in the scrap heap, how much rubber was used . . . but how do you measure a completed performance review process in HR?

Let me share with you what I actually hear from many people on the manufacturing side of business: "I wish our process could talk to us like the processes can in a service environment." I have heard this compared to the difference between a veterinarian and a medical doctor (MD). An MD has the ability to talk to the patient and ask questions that will help in the understanding and diagnosis of the problem. A veterinarian, on the other hand, has to do things more by observation, since the patient cannot articulate what it feels, or help to identify what is wrong.

In short, since a good part of the process in a manufacturing environment cannot "talk" to those trying to improve it, information has to be gathered in other ways. While you may have HR technology that allows you to gather some information *about* your process, you also have access to a wealth of information from the people involved *in* your process—whether they be customers, suppliers, or employees. You simply have to go out and get it!

Voice of the Customer

In the field of quality, the Voice of the Customer (VOC) is a concept that has evolved into a tool: to go out and talk to customers and get a sense from them as to what their needs are. Sounds simple, right? The novelty of the tool is that this is too often *not* done. Plans are made, fixes are created, and operations are improved on assumptive notions of what the customer wants. Sometimes these assumptions are completely accurate, but often they aren't. The best approach is to take that step to engage the customer, and then to gather the highest quality information that can be used in moving forward.

The human resources function does not often *interact* with what would be considered the organization's customer (the consumer of the organization's product or service). HR does, however, have a variety of people and entities that consume HR's services, who are referred to as *internal customers*. There are also entities outside the organization, such as HR service vendors and job applicants, who are considered *external customers*.

The term *stakeholder* is also used by some to refer to line-managers, employees, other departments (finance, IT, facilities, etc.), senior management, and the Board of Directors, shareholders, vendors and suppliers, and the community-at-large. Even though HR may not interact directly with the organization's customers, it is important to think about them as a customer or stakeholder as well.

Since the customer of the organization is probably not one that will be confused with HR's internal and external customers in our discussions, we will primarily use the term customer throughout, but realize that stakeholder is a perfectly acceptable term for you to utilize instead.

In any case, identifying HR's customers (or stakeholders) can be a bit confusing as we pile the multitude of internal and external customers together and present an overwhelming case for serving them all collectively. What must be done is to look at the overall needs of each group of customers, next to divide-and-conquer by interacting with each based on the relevance to the particular process you are looking at, and then to gather the appropriate information about their needs and concerns.

The Conflicting Needs of HR's Customers

Not only does HR have multiple customers with different requirements, but frequently these requirements are in direct conflict with each other (e.g., hiring managers who want exhaustive searches done to find the best candidates vs. senior management who wants to control recruiting expenses). So how do you keep all of these customers satisfied, loyal even? The makeup of the situation is one that often has political ramifications within the organization. There must be a certain acceptance that *you will not be able to keep everyone optimally happy*. The challenge here is to find a balance between available resources, conflicting needs, and, ultimately, what is best for the organization.

Unlike external customers, internal customers may display more of a sense of empathy for the conflicting needs of other internal customers and an appreciation of the limited resources that they might have. This does not mean that excuses will be embraced, but an understanding of how the organization works and an appreciation of the teamwork mentality may help. An external customer, on the other hand, may not care or want to even hear about the needs of your other customers.

This is a delicate area, because HR needs to make sure that it is not pointing to the bureaucracy of the organization in order to engender the trust of the customer (e.g., "There just is not anything I can do . . . you know how it is!").

Wants, Needs, and "Nice-to-Haves"

Once the customer has expressed what his wants are, you will need to look at these carefully and understand which are *needs* and which are *nice-to-haves.* This cannot be discerned arbitrarily by the service provider ("I know what they need . . . even if they don't!"), but it needs to be determined by the customer. This can be accomplished by a process of triangulation and weighting items accordingly, which can easily be done through a process of forced ranking and by asking additional question to contextualize the customer's answers.

The Customer says . . .	I need A I need B I need C I need D
You can then ask a series of questions to contextualize each answer:	Which is more important, A or B? Which is more important, C or D? Why do you need C? What would happen if you didn't get B?

You can then establish which are most important and why, and then you can begin to classify them as *Wants, Needs, and Nice-to-Haves.*

Wants	I need B
	I need D
Needs	I need A
Nice-to-Have	I need C

Critical To Quality Factors (CTQs)

There are certain key inputs in a process that have a definitive impact on the process outputs. Better management of these inputs will help ensure the process has a reduction in defects. It is imperative to convert customer needs and wants into specific and measurable requirements for the business to implement. These are called Critical to Quality factors or CTQs.

Customer needs are the broad elements that make up customer requirements. From these needs, we can understand what the drivers are that influence those needs. For example:

An HR department was receiving a significant number of complaints regarding its benefits enrollment process. By analyzing the customer survey data and developing the CTQ Tree (see the following page), the business was able to identify critical-to-satisfaction requirements. These requirements became the focus for improving customer satisfaction. The HR department eliminated the mandatory benefits enrollment meetings and made the information available online in an e-learning format with shorter sections available that addressed different benefit areas. Eliminating the long mandatory meetings satisfied the customers who had relatively simple benefits and allowed them to quickly find the information that was applicable just to them. A Frequently Asked Questions feature was updated in real time to address questions as they came up. For those employees who did not check the FAQ center, they were able to email questions to the HR department, which responded within 24 hours.

The objective is to take a general, difficult-to-measure need (i.e., to improve homeowner warranty satisfaction) and develop specific, measurable, and actionable requirements to drive improvements in customer satisfaction.

Creating a CTQ Tree

1. List each need from the customer's point of view
2. Ask "What would that mean?" about each need
3. These become drivers
4. Keep asking "What that would mean?" until a measurable CTQ is identified.

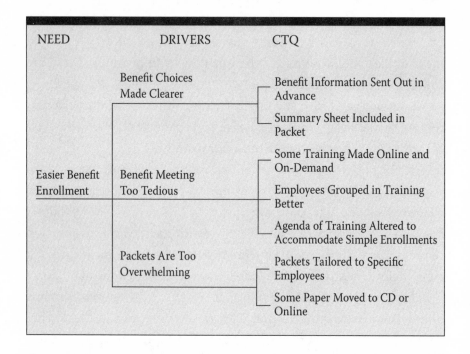

NEED	DRIVERS	CTQ
	Benefit Choices Made Clearer	Benefit Information Sent Out in Advance
		Summary Sheet Included in Packet
Easier Benefit Enrollment	Benefit Meeting Too Tedious	Some Training Made Online and On-Demand
		Employees Grouped in Training Better
		Agenda of Training Altered to Accommodate Simple Enrollments
	Packets Are Too Overwhelming	Packets Tailored to Specific Employees
		Some Paper Moved to CD or Online

◄───►

General   **Specific**

(Hard to Measure)   (Easy to Measure)

FIGURE 3-1

CTQ Tree: A tool that aids in translating customer language into quantified requirements for your product or service.

Why create a CTQ Tree:

- It helps translate broad customer requirements into specific critical-to-quality (CTQ) requirements

- It helps the team to move from high-level to detailed specifications

- It ensures that all aspects of the need are identified.

Use a CTQ Tree to determine:

- Unspecified customer requirements

- Complex, broad needs.

Gathering Voice of the Customer Information

There are several different ways to gather Voice of the Customer information, all of which have pros and cons. These range from surveys to focus groups to one-on-one meetings, all of which bring different levels of information and carry with them different levels of cost. Overall, I recommend a tiered approach: utilize several tools to gather different levels of information (e.g., focus groups, then a larger survey, followed by personal interviews). This will, of course, depend on the size of your organization. If the number of customers that you have is small enough, then you can gather information from all of them directly without investing too much in the way of resources. Remember that the quality of information you get from interviews will depend on the skill of the interviewer and the questions asked. While the interview need not be overly structured, it is important for it not to have too lackadaisical of a tone to it. Casually opening a dialogue may help to establish rapport but fail to contribute much in the way of useful information.

Start with a handful of one-on-one meetings to help you understand some of the key issues. This will allow you to create a structure that can be used to facilitate one or several focus group meetings. From these focus groups, key issues to address can be identified and taken to the general employee population for validation through surveys. I don't recommend a survey that becomes a blind fishing expedition for information. While you can go back and reconvene meetings with individuals or focus groups, repeating surveys to the general employee population is not advisable unless you're doing a quarterly or annual follow-up to gauge progress.

One other way to gather information is simply by observation. This used to be called *management by walking around.* Observing the customer can take many forms, both in person and online. In person could be in the form of observing candidates interviewing at the organization and whether they seem frustrated or impressed, or seem more interested in getting out of there! Without taking on too much of a Big Brother persona, customers also can be studied online through their activities. For example, on which spot of the company Intranet do employees spend most of their time? Is it looking at explanations of benefits? Another example would be looking at the path followed by an online job-seeker. Usage reports are normally easily generated by your IT staff and these reports can tell you a great deal about the path that online job-seekers follow when they come to your site. This can help you identify their areas of interest, as well their *exit pages,* which are the pages that job-seekers most often exit out of as they leave your site. From this, you can triangulate when and why job-seekers leave.

Your IT staff or webmaster probably has access to a wealth of information that can provide historical reports and ongoing information to help fine-tune online HR initiatives. You need to ask, though!

For example, ask what information you can get about:
- Traffic to your career or job section on your website
  - What positions were most viewed?
  - What is the ratio of jobs viewed to jobs applied for?
  - How many people quit in the middle of the application process?
- Employee traffic to HR information portals
  - What sections are used most?

• Is there a time when information is accessed most frequently?
• How much time do employees spend there?

This type of information could be used to optimize e-HR initiatives. But first you must gather the information and take the time to understand what it means.

Summary of the Primary Methods to
Gather Voice of the Customer Information

Interviews

This is the primary method by which VOC is often gathered. In addition to the benefit of building rapport with the customer, interviews should be utilized to identify issues and to explore known issues more deeply. The quality of the data gathered depends upon the skill of the interviewer.

Focus Groups

These involve getting a selected number of managers, employees, department representatives, or some other collection of customers together to answer questions in a group setting. Focus groups can help identify issues for further study by posing follow-up questions to other members and to the group as a whole, based on responses given. Like interviews, the quality of data is determined by the skill of the interviewer, and strong facilitation skills need to be present to keep the activity productive as well as for general "crowd control."

Surveys

Surveys can be utilized to gather data to frame known issues and look at progress of improvements over time. They allow the reliability of responses to be improved by increasing the number of respondents, but surveys can be expensive and cumbersome to do.

Complaints

Tracking complaints and analyzing them for common denominators and potential root causes can be a very useful endeavor. While sexual harassment and other claims are often dealt with in a very formal manner, HR is normally not as precise about logging and tracking complaints to resolution regarding HR operations or service.

Observation

Watching your customers as they interact with HR and utilize HR services can tell you some things about their experience. This is a helpful initial method to identify VOC issues, but should never be used as a primary source of gathering VOC information.

Technology

Technology (e.g., websites, HRIS, HR Intranet portals) can offer the ability to observe customers and HR employees to spot trends and better understand the usage of HR services. The information can be accessed quickly and relatively inexpensively. (I will discuss more on this in chapters 6 and 10).

Voice of the Customer Questions

Online Resource Center

Here are some examples of questions that can help you draw out the VOC:

1. What are the top two to three HR issues that are important to you?
2. What are the best features of HR's service?
3. In what ways does HR perform well?
4. What part of HR frustrates you?
5. What aspects of HR's service would you strongly recommend we not change?
6. In what areas do outside_____(search firms, trainers, etc.) perform better than our internal _____(recruiters, trainers, etc.)?
7. In what areas can we improve the relationship between our department and your department?
8. If you had a magic wand, what would you change about our service to you, your team, or your department?
9. What services, which you need from us, are you not getting?
10. How does our failure to meet your expectations impact your operation?
11. What services are you getting from us that you do *not* need?
12. How do you see your needs changing in the future?

Frame of Reference—
What Do Good and Bad Look Like?

It is critical to understand the context of responses you get from your customers about the surveys you conduct. Blending qualitative responses with quantitative reports can help you more positively impact your HR performance "metrics."

In asking typical attitudes questions* (Strongly Agree/Agree/ Neutral/Disagree/Strongly Disagree) or standard rating questions (1 to 5, with 5 being Excellent and 1 being Poor), it is helpful to understand what Excellent and Poor look like to the person rating the service. In essence, "What would the experience need to be to have you rate it a 5 (Excellent)? What would cause you to rate the service with a 1 (Poor) rating?"

Gathering these responses and summarizing them can help you to better understand the scores that you do get, and to identify your customers' hot buttons. By sorting these responses into categories, you will be able see the common denominators and thus be better equipped to prioritize your efforts.

Complaints as a Source of VOC Information

Unlike customer complaints that are normally carefully tracked by customer service or marketing departments, complaints about HR service are less likely to be tracked over time. There is usually a less formalized procedure for dealing with complaints as they come in. Part of this has to do with the internal customer aspect of complaints—that is, co-workers or internal customers are often less blunt about lodging complaints. A manager might be called or something might be said to an intermediary. There is less likelihood that the issue will turn into a formal complaint because of internal culture issues (i.e., "not getting someone in trouble") and also because of the potential hassle of raising a complaint (having to explain the issue as more people jump into the fray, with the end result that the

---

* These are called Likert Scales.

complaint ends up being more trouble than it is worth). Complaints are also something that do not necessarily come directly to HR or management. They come vertically up the grapevine or are passed along from another department.

The Culture of Complaints

Depending on your organizational culture, internal complaints may be common or nonexistent. This may be influenced by the culture of response to complaints. Is something actually done when complaints are voiced? As time goes on, it is common for internal cultures to wear down the interest in complaints by inaction. People think, "Why bother?" While some individuals don't think that not complaining will help the situation, they don't have faith that complaining will either. This culture can influence smaller issues such as not having your phone calls returned, to significant issues such as not reporting cases of sexual harassment. The best approach is to reaffirm the open lines of communication and your willingness to take action. If you sense any kind of frustration, pro-actively going to the source and asking some Voice of the Customer questions can help you draw out the information.

It is a common adage that for every one customer that complains, countless more do not—or if they do, it is often not to you. Inside an organization, this can have a negative infectious effect on the reputation of an internal department such as human resources.

Voice of the Customer: Qualitative Data

The combination of quantitative information as well as the qualitative intelligence that can be gathered through the human process of discovery will add to overall results.

However, it is important to remember to keep the focus on the customer and not just on the data.

Sometimes it is also important to gather triangulated information about a particular department—that means talking to more than just the manager or director. Speaking to individuals at different levels within this part of the organization can be very enlightening. This can mean speaking to the administrative assistant of that executive, as well as to other direct reports. You'll often find that their needs are expressed quite differently than those of the executive. What they believe that the department needs will often be colored mostly by their function in the department.

Good qualitative data can be the result of in-depth interviewing that concentrates on the depth of feelings expressed rather than the number of responses. This is a process of asking the right questions, and being willing not just to hear, but to listen to, a customer—even if you're not always hearing what you would like to hear.

Conceptual Questions

What are your major challenges?

What are the biggest changes you face?

What changes have you seen in your boss's expectations in the last six months? Year? Two years?

What changes have you seen in your customers' expectations in the last six months? Year? Two years?

Gather anecdotes and stories that help you illustrate the underlying issues. These may not necessarily put a specific face on the problem, but they help humanize it so that others can understand it better.

Gather Frame of Reference Questions

- Overall, how would you characterize your relationship with the human resources departments at all of the organizations where you've worked?

- What do you see is the number-one way that HR can help you?

- Who do you think gets more focus or attention from HR than you do?

Conducting a Qualitative Interview

Set ground rules by telling participants:

- Who the interviewer is

- What's going to happen

- Why it is important

- How they (the customers) were chosen

- What will happen with the data or information (and when)

- The confidentiality of the interview

- How long it will take.

Follow Up

Once all the notes of the interview have been transcribed, it is important to review it with those who provided the information. This will allow you to verify whether the interview was on target. Besides checking the validity of the information gathered, this also serves to increase confidence on the part of the interviewee with the process and to reinforce that they were actually heard. This also forces them to take ownership of what was said (even though confidentiality may still play a role here).

Making Sense of All of Your
Voice of the Customer Information

In order to objectively and methodically analyze quality data, a categorizing or *affinity process* must take place.

As you begin to organize responses and sound bites, you need to put them into groups by their theme or area. So, for example, all comments about making a form simpler would be grouped together for easier review. This will allow reviewers to see the clustering of comments together and help them to recognize any common denominators. Obviously, certain responses will need to be edited without losing their intended meaning. This may need to happen in the data gathering stage rather than in the data cleanup stage. That is to say, encapsulating the response from an interviewee can help understanding, and it will provide a more usable sound bite that summarizes the issue.

Exact quotes can be transcribed onto a spreadsheet and, out of these, categories can be established. By creating umbrella categories, you will be creating boxes in which to organize the comments. Some comments will be duplicated and put in more than one box. Once the categories have been established, an effective way to validate how the comments are categorized is to give the job to two or more people (or teams) and ask them to categorize the results. The beauty here is that, with a spreadsheet, you can take the category column and simply "cut and paste" the two results next to each other and look for gaps. Ideally, with clearly-defined categories, the efforts of the different groups will, for the most part, *sync* up. If not, it may be necessary to revisit the labels and definitions. Once clear categories are created and qualitative data is sorted accordingly, it is helpful to summarize the comments or describe them in some shortened form.

Notice, you will need to figure out *what is actionable.*

This means that you will need to figure out how this can be translated into both tactical and strategic concerns of the HR department. As this information is relayed to the rest of organization, it may make some people who are not on the primary team gathering information uncomfortable, especially if it relates to their performance. If the information has been gathered in a professional and objective manner, some discomfort on the part of staff is okay. This shouldn't be a comfortable process, since the objective is *to move out of comfort zones and away from what businesses-as-usual has looked like in the past.*

Remember, though, this isn't the Inquisition or a finger-pointing game. This is a *process* to understand where the opportunities for improvement lie so that you and your organization can move toward actually improving the process.

There is a definite danger in washing qualitative data and paring it down to be more palatable in a presentation. Like a gold miner, you will be sifting meticulously through piles of dirt in order to find those few golden nuggets that are invaluable! In addition to categorizing responses, I also recommend having the interviewers identify and briefly talk about the most noteworthy comments, words, tone, or nonverbal responses that they observed. What were the golden nuggets they perceived? This can help others gain the proper perspective, without having been there.

Implicit and Explicit Requirements

We have to think about two elements of the Voice of the Customer: the spoken (explicit) and the unspoken (implicit). A great amount of dissatisfaction on the part of a customer happens when the implicit or unspoken needs are not met. These are often service areas that are simply expected. While most of these are common sense and one would expect you, the service provider, to know and understand them, this may not always be the case. Addressing implicit needs is one of the more insidious aspects of meeting customer requirements. These lapses in service can serve as a surprise to both parties—first, in not having them met, on the part of the customer, and, secondly, not expecting the customer to be upset, on the part of the service provider.

Gathering implicit requirements can take extra effort, but they can be understood by asking more probing questions and by simply observing your customer. Probing questions can be as simple as asking, "What elements of HR's service do you assume and don't feel like you should really have to point out?"

Confidentiality might be an element that managers don't feel the need to state as a requirement, but it could be a source of huge dissatisfaction if it is not met. It is incumbent upon HR to inquire about such implicit requirements. This may prompt mental attention to this issue on the part of the employees and line-managers and allow HR to either identify that confidentiality is not an issue, or provide an opportunity to demonstrate their alignment with the customer's needs for confidentiality. Some other questions that might help deepen the service level and partnership are:

- Are there any walls or resistance that I might run into?

- Is there any sensitivity to this issue?

- How much support do you think this issue has?

- Is there anything else that I either need to know or might be helpful for me to know?

Summary

Look at the customer relationship as having three elements: *meeting customer requirements, exceeding expectations, and anticipating customer needs.* The baseline is, of course, meeting customer requirements. Unless customer requirements are met, anticipating customer needs or exceeding customer expectations will not carry the value that they otherwise would. That is to say that going the "extra mile" or being intuitive are great, but they must come after—and not instead of—the primary focus of meeting customer requirements.

 KEY THOUGHT

Make sure that when you go the extra mile,
it isn't actually a mile out of the way.

4

PROJECT SELECTION
AND CHARTER

When it comes to your product or project,
people will take quality as seriously
as you do—no more so.

(Philip B. "Phil" Crosby, author, 1926–2001)

AFTER identifying your key processes and customers and gathering Voice of the Customer information, you should have a pretty good idea about what areas present opportunities for improvement. In the drive toward excellence, there is a great temptation to try to fix too much too quickly. Like a haphazard plunge into an exercise program, this is a recipe for disaster. Now is the time to make a *strategic* assessment of potential opportunities for improvement. Then, next, to carefully prioritize your future efforts.

It is important to note that an organization's strategic projects *are different from* the operational-improvement projects that are the focus of this book. By focusing first on improving HR operations, the tools you will learn and the experience you will gain will provide the skills that you can then apply to strategic projects throughout your organization.

HR Excellence . . . and World Peace

In any operational excellence endeavor, there is a clear temptation to attempt to fix too much too quickly. These projects are sometimes called "Creating World Peace"—overly ambitious undertakings that are often just too unrealistic in scope. Most are

55

destined to failure, or at least produce lackluster results, because:
- the scope is too large
- the measures of success are poorly defined
- the resources needed are not available
- the skills to effectively do the project are not present
- there is not enough executive-level support in the organization.

For example, creating a project to reduce organization-wide turnover in a multinational company may be difficult, while reducing turnover strictly in the job class of Account Executives is more manageable. Reducing turnover in a company with a few hundred people might also be a manageable project.

Analyzing, Scoring, and Prioritizing Projects

Although there are many ways to evaluate projects, this step is one of the most critical of any quality- or process-improvement initiative. With a finite amount of resources (money, manpower, time) the goal is to allocate them according to the most significant impact to the business. In doing so, an estimate must also be made about the *ability* to execute a plan so that it will achieve the desired impact.

Several areas must be carefully assessed and weighted to objectively prioritize projects. Viability must be considered, and several individual areas must be gauged:

1. Alignment
2. Value and Cost/Benefit
3. Success Probability
4. Availability of Resources.

Alignment	Value and Cost/Benefit
Success Probability	Availability of Resources

These areas can be summarized and given scores to help you gauge projects and to compare different projects to each other, in order to prioritize them, so that there is a maximum probability of success. A sample form is provided in the Online Resource Center.

Alignment	Value and Cost/Benefit
Success Probability	Availability of Resources

ALIGNMENT: PROJECT AREAS

The first question to ask is how a project aligns with the goals and objectives of the business as well as the specific goals and priorities of the HR department. Projects can be separated into three main areas:

- Efficiency
- Customer Service
- Compliance.

Efficiency

This covers two main areas, saving time and saving money:

- Cutting costs
- Eliminating waste
- Streamlining operations
- Reducing head count.

Customer Service

This addresses qualitative service measures, which may be the primary goal of the project, or the ancillary or additional benefits that are gained from efficiency or compliance projects:

- Satisfaction and attitude surveys
- Reduction in complaints
- Changes in the utilization levels of a service (increasing or decreasing with a positive result for the organization)
- Other methods that are not measured through efficiency, but improve the customer experience.

Compliance

This is a risk management category that is a catchall for complying with an organization's rules and regulations and any other issues that could result in some sort of lawsuit, fine, or other liability. Examples are:

- Safety
  - OSHA
  - Workman's Compensation
  - Union
- Security
- Employee Privacy Rights
- Government Reporting
  - Sarbanes Oxley (404)
  - EEO
- Employment laws
  - Discrimination
  - Sexual Harassment
  - ADA
  - FMLA
  - HIPAA

A Note on Efficiency

Making a department more efficient is something that is going to need to be quantified and realized in the form of some sort of tangible savings—otherwise it may fall under a customer service issue.

To clarify, lightening the workload of a department is a noble pursuit, but unless it translates into some financial benefit in terms of eliminating expenses around rework or a reduction in head count, many senior executives will not acknowledge the cost savings.

Project Alignment Example:

Reducing the disparately high turnover of African American employees that was identified in a diversity initiative. Depending on the circumstances, this project could be classified as all three project areas:

- **Efficiency:** eliminating the costs of turnover
- **Customer Service:** improving satisfaction of African American employees, their managers, and all others affected by the turnover
- **Compliance:** addressing a possible compliance issue (EEO or other).

Alignment	Value and Cost/Benefit
Success Probability	Availability of Resources

VALUE AND COST/BENEFIT:
THE BUSINESS CASE FOR A PROJECT

Making the business case for a project includes reviewing the financial viability of a project and:

- The options to consider.

- The costs of the different options—both initial and ongoing. For example, in addition to the initial investment in HR technology, estimated training, maintenance, and future labor support should be considered.

- What changes will occur by implementing the options? These may include both positive and negative changes that result from each option.

- Realistic estimates of the benefits* and effective measurements for these outcomes. This includes the intangible benefits, which may need to be quantified if they are to be given the proper weight that corresponds to the value to the organization.

A business case can be tricky and may not always take into account the value of these non-financial aspects to a project, such as improved customer service or employee satisfaction. These need to be gauged carefully along with strategic concerns for the business and how the project factors into these areas.

---

* A benefit may be in the form of a financial return or the *avoidance* of a financial cost (e.g., lost productivity, fines, lawsuits, turnover, etc.).

Return on Investment Worksheet

Project value and cost/benefit may be judged through a variety of methods, and your senior management will have some method that they use to judge projects in other areas of the business. Net Present Value (NPV) is a common way to judge the Return on Investment of a project.

 A template is provided for you at the Online Resource Center in MS Excel® format as well as instructions on how to fill it out.

Alignment	Value and Cost/Benefit
Success Probability	Availability of Resources

SUCCESS PROBABILITY

While many things *should* be done, the question arises as to what can be done and a lot of this depends on the project's chance for success. The likelihood of project success needs to be objectively looked at and considered, and must be weighed carefully in conjunction with the Value and Cost/Benefit analysis. A project that has high potential value but a marginal likelihood of success should be given heavy scrutiny. This ties in with the availability of resources as well. A project that may tap precious resources without a decent likelihood for success may need to be prioritized *behind* other projects.

An important aspect of project success probability includes looking at what might not "go right" in a project. Assessing and managing *risk* can dramatically impact the probability of a project's success.

Build Those Process-Improvement Muscles First

When considering the probability of successful projects, it is important to remember that if formal process-improvement activities have not been an integral part of your HR department's culture and activities, the choices for project selection need to be tempered in light of your ability. That is to say that the most important project, whether it is where there is the most pain or the most opportunity for gain, may not be the best place to start. Like our exercise program analogy, jumping into advanced exercises without first properly conditioning and building up your muscles is not only a path to being sore, but possibly one that leads to injury, and one that may lead to your need to abandon the exercise routine altogether. With respect to picking projects, it is important to build up your process-improvement muscles and learn the different tools that you will use on an ongoing basis to improve operations.

Alignment	Value and Cost/Benefit
Success Probability	Availability of Resources

AVAILABILITY OF RESOURCES

One of the key constraints factoring into project selection is the issue of finite resources; you simply cannot fix everything at once because there simply is not the time, staff, and/or budget. This makes resource availability a critical issue to consider in project selection.

If effective value of a project is established and the cost/benefit has been carefully weighed, you are significantly closer to getting the resources needed to complete necessary projects—even when you do not currently have the budget to do so. Having created the business case, budget can often be "found" in the organization in the short term to fund a project.

Depending on the nature of the project, your management may be more or less stringent about the self-sustainability or ability of a project to quickly return the initial investment in resources through cost savings. Correcting a compliance issue is necessary, of course, but since no money was budgeted for the fines that non-compliance would create, the demonstration of a project paying for itself becomes more problematic. This returns us to the necessity of building a "good business" case for a project.

Manpower and Getting Help

There is nothing that says you must handle this process-improvement effort by yourself. Draw on whatever talent can be rallied from within your organization to assist in project management, statistical, or financial analysis—even graphic design of a process map is something that very well might be done more quickly and better by someone else on staff or by a contractor.

Your goal is to improve departmental well being, not to become an expert at statistics or designing flowcharts. With that in mind, strike a balance of learning curves and delegation.

As tasks come up, consider that the best match of skills compatible with pending tasks might come from outside the HR department. If your business case is strong enough, senior management can often help cut through any organizational "silos" to help you get assistance in some form.

The Project Charter

As you begin your first project, it is important to set it up for success. A key element of a successful project is a clear *project charter.* This is a document that summarizes the key elements, and should include:

Project Justification	Why must this project take place?
Process Importance	Why is this process important? What is/are cause(s) for the prioritization of this project?
Process Problems	What needs to be fixed?
Project Objective	What is the purpose of the project?
Project Scope	What is the project supposed to accomplish? And, perhaps equally important, what is it not supposed to accomplish?
Project Deliverables	What will the project produce? (Will it be a new, streamlined process? A form? Information?)
Assumptions/ Limitations	Is the project based on any assumptions about the business? About the market environment?
Team Members	Who will work on the project? (There must be a Project Manager or leader of the other project team members. Subject Matter Experts (SMEs) may also be involved at different parts of the project, but are not team members that will be involved throughout the entire life-cycle of the project.)
Time Frame (including Start Date, End Date, and Milestones)	The project must have a definitive start and end date, just as it must have a scope. Otherwise, projects lack a sense of urgency and often stretch on into the future without gaining enough momentum to yield results. The end date may be just an estimate and as time goes on you will become more adept at gauging the time a project will take.

Project Charter	
Project Title: Staffing Process Improvement	

Project Leader: Patricia Williams – Staffing Manager	**Team Members:** Debbie Jones - HR Director

	Jim Smith – HR Generalist
Stakeholders: All hiring managers/departments Candidates/Applicants Senior Management	Dana Andrews – Sr. Recruiter Mike Fort – HRIS Specialist Martin Livingston – CFO (Project Sponsor)

Problem/Opportunity Statement	**Business Case**
Hiring managers, candidates and applicants have expressed dissatisfaction with the employment process. Senior management is examining the use of budget for staffing and considering exploring outsourcing part or all of staffing.	Efficient and effective staffing is a critical activity for the sustainability of the organization. The use of third-party recruiting firms has become cost prohibitive and the overall quality of hires needs to be improved to reduce turnover and improve organizational performance.
Project Objective	**Deliverables**
The objective of this project is to recommend improvements and/or changes to the staffing processes that will: • Improve quality of service • Improve client satisfaction • Ensure efficient use of time and resources by establishing, or refining process metrics.	Each process will be mapped and documented. Specific improvements will be documented and action plans agreed to and implemented. Metrics will be established to measure improvements in areas identified.
Project Scope	**Assumptions/Limitations**
The staffing processes all typically begin with the identification of a job vacancy and end when an individual has reported to work. The project will focus on the following staffing and employment processes: • Non-exempt external hiring • Exempt level external recruiting • College Recruiting for regular positions Scope of work does not include summer intern hiring or internal exempt level hiring.	The organization has planned annual growth of approximately 10% of the employee base in addition to replacement of any turnover.

Timeframe	Target Date	Actual Date
Project Start	10/30/07	
Define	11/13/07	
Measure	12/18/07	
Analyze	1/15/08	
Improve	2/5/08	
Control	2/19/08	
Project Complete	2/26/08	
Future Review Date	8/26/08	

Project Charter and Project Selection templates are available in the Online Resource Center.

MEASURE

Before you can improve operations, you must understand them and be able to measure them. If it can be measured, it can be improved.

First, you must be able to articulate what the process is, and that can be accomplished through process mapping. Once you understand your processes, you can establish how and where to effectively measure them. From this, you can create a baseline to be used to mark the starting point from which you will gauge improvements.

PROCESS MAPPING

METRICS

Define   Measure   Analyze   Improve   Control

PROCESS MAPPING

*A good plan is like a road map: it shows the final destination
and usually the best way to get there.*

(H. Stanley Judd, author)

Now I will explore process mapping as a tool for process
analysis and management. I will begin by discussing the
difference between flowcharting and process mapping, and
will then move on to examine the different stages of process mapping.

Process mapping can be an invaluable step toward excellence.
Although to some, process mapping may seem like a tedious exercise in the pursuit of excellence in HR, it can be one of the most
useful activities you do. Process mapping serves several purposes,
including:

- Helping to understand the big picture
- Illustrating the difference between how it is *thought* a
  process is done and how it *really* is done
- Identifying the cross-functional path a process may take
- Breaking a process down into phases
- Helping to identify timing and resources needs
- Identifying where to measure a process to manage its
  results.

Once you have created a process map and used it internally within
the HR department to improve your operations, it can then be used
outside the HR department when discussing your processes as a:

• Visual aid
• Training tool
• Simple project management plan.

There is also a historical legacy of sorts which the process map creates by memorializing how things are currently done. This can last on through shifts in management personnel, through mergers and acquisitions, and during the transition to outsourcing (and, even more critically, when an outsourced process must be brought back in-house due to poor quality or service).

What Is a Process Map?

A process map is a graphical representation of a process. It is sometimes referred to as a flowchart, but a flowchart is more specifically just the graphical representation of a series of *steps*. (See Figure 5-1 for a comparison.) A process map uses the tools of flowcharting, but can go beyond them to describe more about a process (e.g., who performs specific steps in the process). A process map may represent several sub-processes that comprise an overall process. The more complex the process, the more extensive the map or diagram will be.

Flowchart: A graphical representation of a series of steps using certain symbols to represent events.

Process map: a graphical representation of a process that may look at any number of things including inputs, outputs, measures, and how a process follows a non-linear path between departments and participants.

How do I know which is which? A process map tells more about a process than just the simple steps in a process, such as who perfiorms a particular task. Also, a flowchart normally reads from top to bottom, and a process map often reads from left to right.

The Macro and the Detailed

A SIPOC drawing helps us understand the big picture of a process and outlines the key phases and what the inputs and outputs are in a particular process. Flowcharts and process maps can represent a big picture view of things (macro), but process maps can chart out the very detailed parts of a process. The information on a detailed process map can then be analyzed to understand:

• Where inputs enter the process

• Where outputs are created (data, completed forms, records)

• Where and how to measure the process to gain useful information about its functioning.

Below are examples of frequently used flowcharts and process maps.

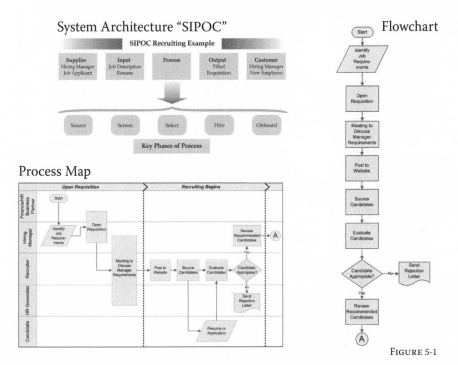

FIGURE 5-1

A process chart by its very nature includes both macro and detailed information. The following figure shows how the flow of information shapes your process mapping.

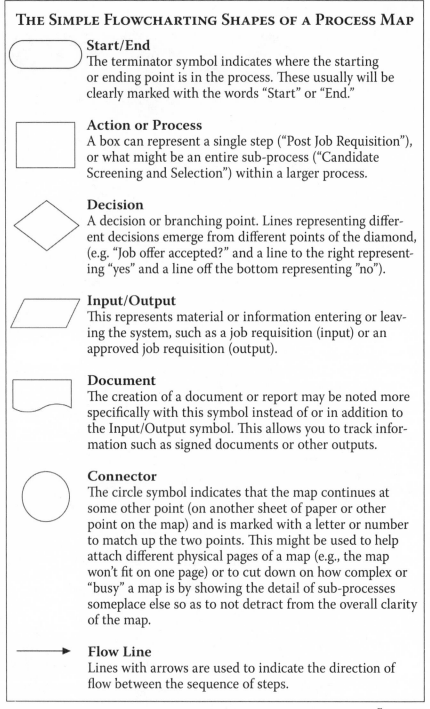

THE SIMPLE FLOWCHARTING SHAPES OF A PROCESS MAP

Start/End
The terminator symbol indicates where the starting or ending point is in the process. These usually will be clearly marked with the words "Start" or "End."

Action or Process
A box can represent a single step ("Post Job Requisition"), or what might be an entire sub-process ("Candidate Screening and Selection") within a larger process.

Decision
A decision or branching point. Lines representing different decisions emerge from different points of the diamond, (e.g. "Job offer accepted?" and a line to the right representing "yes" and a line off the bottom representing "no").

Input/Output
This represents material or information entering or leaving the system, such as a job requisition (input) or an approved job requisition (output).

Document
The creation of a document or report may be noted more specifically with this symbol instead of or in addition to the Input/Output symbol. This allows you to track information such as signed documents or other outputs.

Connector
The circle symbol indicates that the map continues at some other point (on another sheet of paper or other point on the map) and is marked with a letter or number to match up the two points. This might be used to help attach different physical pages of a map (e.g., the map won't fit on one page) or to cut down on how complex or "busy" a map is by showing the detail of sub-processes someplace else so as to not detract from the overall clarity of the map.

Flow Line
Lines with arrows are used to indicate the direction of flow between the sequence of steps.

FIGURE 5-2

**Flowchart
Example of
a Process
Map**

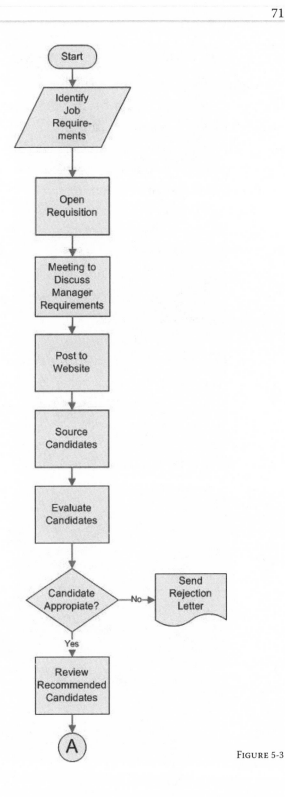

FIGURE 5-3

Cross-Functional or Swim Lane Maps

Another form of process mapping—the cross-functional map—helps us understand how work is shared among different departments, people, and outside entities. This map is also often referred to as a *swim lane map* because of the way it is set up to show rows that represent people or functions in the organization. These rows look similar to the lanes in a swimming pool.

The swim lane map demonstrates how work often does not flow in a straight, linear fashion, but moves in a zigzag pattern, with many contributors taking part in moving the process from start to finish.

To identify when work moves into the area of a contributor, we create lines on the process map to represent the swim lanes. Swim lanes act as visual rows to allow the user to quickly identify:

- *Who* is involved in the process
- *What* steps of the process they are involved in
- *When* exactly they are involved
- *Where* in the overall flow of the process they are involved.

Swim Lane Map of a Recruiting Process

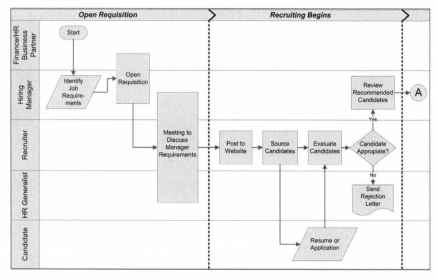

FIGURE 5-4

Reading a Swim Lane Map

The swim lane map has a couple of new aspects to it as compared to a simple flowchart. If a task sits in a particular swim lane, it means that entity (person, department, vendor, etc.) does that task. But what if more than one swim lane is involved in a task?

Shapes Spanning across Lanes

To demonstrate that more than one person, department, or entity will take part in that step, flowcharting shapes representing that step are stretched to span between swim lanes. (See Figure 5-4.)

Shapes Skipping across Lanes

As shapes span across lanes, they may need to skip a lane because a particular swim lane is not involved in a step, i.e., their swim lane happens to sit between those that are involved. Rather than making two shapes that could falsely indicate two steps or separate tasks, the shape is stretched across between the two lanes furthest apart, and the lanes that are in-between but not involved are indicated with a dashed line and/or different shading. (See Figure 5-5.)

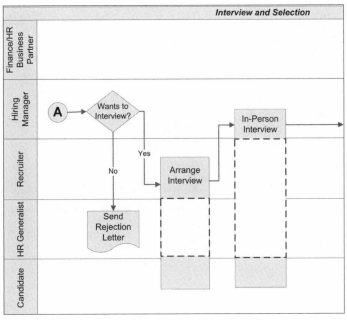

FIGURE 5-5

Current State and Desired State

Ultimately, there are at least two different process maps that you will need to create: 1) what the *current* process looks like (the current state) and 2) what the process will *ideally* look like after improvements are made (the desired state). From these, the discrepancies can be identified and steps taken to correct them.

Once you have moved into the *Improve* section where possible improvements are identified through technology, outsourcing, or other streamlining efforts, you will create a *new* map that identifies the desired state and actually shows these improvements. Once your improvements are complete, the *desired* state map will become your *new working* map of the process that you can use in your day-to-day operations to illustrate how the process functions.

Process Mapping Software

Initially, process maps can be drawn on paper or a whiteboard, but the preferred way to document a process map is with process mapping software. This will make the process of making changes and the creation of current and future state maps a dynamic and fluid process.

A flowchart can be made with text boxes and the line tool in Microsoft Word®, but if there is any complexity to your diagram this could very easily make you crazy when trying to rearrange items and reconnect the boxes. The beauty of flowcharting software, in addition to the ready-made templates, is that the flow lines between items (the lines with arrows) are *dynamic* and will update as you drag and move things around.

You already may be familiar with these concepts from your use of organization charting software—which may have flowcharting capabilities that you can adapt for process mapping.

Process Mapping vs. Process Drawing

Let us take a moment to clarify the difference between mapping and drawing. Process mapping is the task of identifying and understanding the events that take place in a process.

Process drawing is the physical illustration of a process: putting it down on paper or in a software program. Though the drawing part can be complex depending on the process you are representing and the tool you use, it is only the physical representation of all the work that went before it.

This can be likened to the fact that writing with the use of a word processing program does not make you a good writer, but only helps in putting the material in electronic written form. So knowing MS Word® will not help you write a good business plan any more than owning a scalpel makes you a brain surgeon. The same goes for the use of flowcharting and process mapping software. The real work will not be in learning the software, but in working through the understanding of your processes.

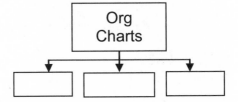

Quick Tip

If you currently create your organization charts in MS Word®, PowerPoint® or some other software, you should definitely explore MS Visio® or Smartdraw®. These programs can also dynamically create and update organizational charts from data directly from your HRIS or a spreadsheet, and create organizational hierarchies with the following four fields: name, title, department, and supervisor.

Investing in Flowcharting Software

Some examples of popular flowcharting software packages are:

- Visio® (Microsoft)   www.microsoft.com/visio
- Flowcharter (iGrafx)®   www.igrafx.com
- Smartdraw®   www.smartdraw.com

When choosing flowcharting software, keep in mind a couple things:

- What, if any, flowcharting software is already in use in your company? (e.g., the IT department is a common place to look for flowcharting software already in place).

- How can your flowcharting software be utilized for other HR functions, such as organization charts, office floor plan mapping, etc.?

- If you have existing organization charting software, does it have flowcharting capabilities?

- Important: These programs can often be tried at no charge for 30 days. But choose carefully among these free trials, because your work and learning curve are parts of the investment. Fortunately, the major packages are getting better about importing from other packages, but check this before you decide on a package so that you will not have your work trapped in a software package that you will be stuck with.

Everyone Doesn't Need It!

In addition to the learning curve of using the software, there is the expense of the software license itself. Visio®, iGraphix®, and Smartdraw® have created read-only software that is available for free so that team members without a license for the full drawing software can view and print flowchart diagrams—without having to get them in Portable Document Format (PDF), such as Adobe Acrobat®, or some other form. Go to your process mapping software's website to check for free reader software for team members.

Quick Tip

See below for how to locate flowcharting and simple Process Drawing in Microsoft Word®, Excel®, PowerPoint®, and Publisher®.

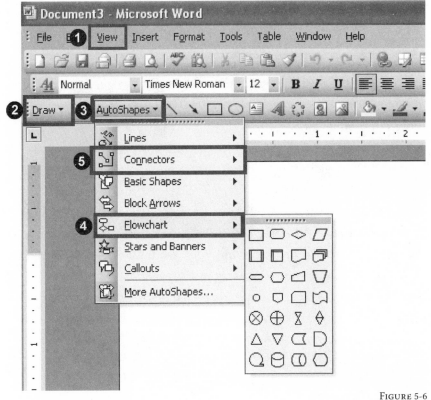

FIGURE 5-6

There are *basic* flowcharting tools built into Microsoft Word®, Excel®, PowerPoint®, and Publisher®!

If you go to View > Toolbars (1) and show the Drawing Toolbar (2), you can use two areas in the AutoShapes (3) pull-down menu: the Flowchart symbols (4) and the Connectors (5).

See the Online Resource Center for a brief tutorial if you need additional instruction.

To Map or Not To Map . . . Is NOT the Question!

You may be asking yourself, "Is process mapping something that we should do?"

The answer is "yes," and the only real question should be: "In *how much detail* do we map our processes?"

Detailed process mapping can be a task that can take up hundreds of man-hours, depending on the complexity of your processes and how detailed you make your mapping. Not every process may be worth mapping out in detail, but you can reduce layers of potential inefficiency by clearing out and honing your proposed process at the more detailed level.

The best plan of attack is to map your key processes at a macro level and then drill down deeper based on where there is the most pain, and where the best opportunities are for improvement.

Taking the time to carefully map your processes will help you later on at many different stages in your efforts to improve your process. And it will help you and your team to understand and be able to *think* about your processes in a visual context. The degree of detail you will need really depends on what you are trying to accomplish in your improvement efforts, and you will need to create your maps accordingly.

 **KEY THOUGHTS**

- Process mapping is a critical activity to help you understand your processes in a visual manner so they can be analyzed and improved.

- Process mapping allows you to create a reference point as you move from where your processes are (current state) to where you would like them to be after you improve them (desired state).

METRICS AND PROCESS MEASUREMENT

*Data is like garbage. You'd better be sure what you're
going to do with it before you collect it.*

(Mark Twain, author, 1835–1910 [apocryphal])

G ATHERING business-performance measurements, which are
commonly called *metrics*, has presented a particular
challenge to HR professionals. Even though HR industry
thought leader Jac Fitz-enz wrote How to *Measure Human Resources*
in 1984 (an industry standard when it comes to HR metrics the-
ory), measuring certain aspects of HR's performance—especially
the qualitative aspects of human resources—still perplex many HR
professionals.

Metrics, Metrics, Metrics . . . Now What?

No one in our industry doubts that there has been considerable
discussion about the importance of metrics in HR. As an industry, it
is more critical than ever for us to get into a better habit of meticulously tracking the work that we do. This is necessary to demonstrate
our successes and to build cases for change. (Note: As we get better and better at effectively tracking metrics, we will also build a
historical perspective that gives us a frame of reference to measure
against, e.g., internal benchmarking.)

After we've gathered this data, the next step looming ahead of us is to align these metrics with our business goals to create change. In essence, we are moving toward both accurately keeping score and having a frame of reference via historical tracking.

After that, the next step is to actively try to improve our future scores.

In the meantime, we need to look at the process metrics that will show us how we can arrive at these scores. This is the subject of the material below.

Death by Metrics

Measuring your processes can be done in such time-consuming detail that it could well replace your full-time duties in human resources!

Though there are worthwhile benefits, a key issue to consider is the short-term impact of measuring productivity by taking time away from work to do measurement. There is a distinct drain in productivity that occurs by having to stop what you are *doing* to *measure* what you are doing.

Therefore, a balance must be maintained between your primary duties and the time invested in measurement.

Dashboard Metrics vs. Process Metrics

I want to differentiate between what are commonly referred to as dashboard metrics and organizational scorecard numbers from the gathering of more specific process metrics. To clarify, dashboard metrics are a smaller number of metrics that represent key performance indicators of HR operations. These are broad measurements such as turnover, cost-per-hire, benefits expenditures per employee, etc. These may also be even higher level numbers (organizational scorecard numbers) which look at the overall performance of the organization.

As there has been a wealth of information written about these "big-picture" metrics in HR, the focus of this next segment will be on the measurement of your processes and their specific aspects in order to help you improve them.

While dashboard metrics are important for keeping an eye on your operations, we are going to "look under the hood." This will entail gathering data that may not be as readily available or something you cannot just extract from existing spreadsheets; it is information you are going to have to go out and get. And, it is information that you most likely did not gather in the past, because you were not looking this closely at your processes.

Process Metrics

Since you are measuring a service and not a product, it becomes more difficult to establish standards of measurement and to create tools to get the information that you need. These measures may come from a:

- Check sheet or daily log
- Spreadsheet or other report
- Human Resource Information System (HRIS).

The most basic part of your initial measurement is the check sheet or daily log. This can be in electronic form, but it could also be in as simple a form as a piece of paper with marks to represent transactions. A daily log can be created in real time or it can be created at the end of the day (e.g., looking at your received and sent emails daily to determine which ones were regarding benefits questions). Even in large organizations with complex systems and HR call centers that measure call times and log every transaction, a check sheet may be necessary to document what isn't tracked at the time, such as tracking a specific issue that is now coming up repeatedly. The electronic form of the check sheet could be in the form of creating an optional field in a database to identify and count a transaction.

Types of Measures

There are four general types of process measures:

- Input
- Activity
- Output
- Outcome.

These measures are at the heart of the SIPOC diagram we looked at in chapter 2: the inputs, process/activity, and outputs. The more elusive measure on our list, the fourth and final one, is the one often not asked: What is the outcome of our activity? What are we trying to accomplish by doing it? Ultimately, most processes in business are not done to create an output but, rather, to create an *outcome*. For example, a completed recruiting requisition is not the desired outcome of a recruiting process: *it is the hiring of a new employee.*

Measure Type	Example
Input	Number of recruiter hours
Activity	Number of recruiting requisitions worked on
Output	Hires made
Outcome	Percent achievement of actual head count to budgeted head count.

GATHERING MEANINGFUL DATA

As you think about measuring your data, you will need to address the following questions:

- What measures are going to be used?
- What is the method of measurement?
- How repeatable is the method of measurement?
- Does the method of measurement exhibit any bias?

What Measures Are Going to Be Used?

As you look at what to measure, it all comes back to measuring what is important to your customers. So what are the Key Customer Requirements? What are the Critical to Quality inputs? This is where you will look at your detailed process maps and identify:

- Inputs
- Activities
- Outputs
- Outcomes.

As you look at these, you can measure several things. For example:

- Number of outputs created
- Ratios to HR people (of activities, outputs, etc.)
- Time measurements (total cycle time or measurements of key steps that are CTQs—e.g., the time to respond to an employee benefits question or the time to reprocess and deliver an incorrect paycheck).

What Is the Method of Measurement?

You must understand how you will gather your measurements. Some questions to ask yourself are:

- Will it be measured manually, such as by a check sheet that is filled out by staff members?
- Or, will technology be used to gather it?
- Or, will someone gather it from other reports or other forms of measure like surveys, exit interviews, spreadsheets, and reports?
- Will all of the data be gathered or will a sample (part of) the total data be used to generalize to the entire population?

Sampling

Depending on the size of your organization and the number of process transactions you are looking at, sampling may be necessary to gather information in an economical manner. This means using a smaller part of the total of your data or transactions and looking at it/them as a way to generalize and draw conclusions about the total. Sampling can be randomly generated (e.g., every 10th employee ID in the HRIS), or drawn from some other method that pulls out a group that represents the population (e.g., one week's or one month's worth of data to generalize about a larger time period). How many should that be? That depends on how confident you want to be in your results. The larger the sample, the more confident you can be in generalizing to the population.

See the Online Resource Center for a calculator to help you choose a proper sample size.

Online Resource Center

How Repeatable Is the Method of Measurement?

In understanding how repeatable a method of measurement is, you should ask the question: "If we did this again, would we get the same result?" In a service environment, there are often many variables playing into the equation, so an exact duplicate result may not be achievable. What you measure, though, must have some element of common results to make the information useful—i.e., comparing "apples to apples."

Does the Method of Measurement Exhibit Any Bias?

In an effort to gather accurate information, every effort must be taken to remove bias from the method of measurement. Though many dieters might think otherwise, a weight scale neither likes nor hates the dieter and does not change its measurement based on bias. However, people often *do exhibit bias* in their measurement, and the best way to limit this is to use clear definitions, and to develop a way to standardize data so as to properly classify it.

The Hawthorne Effect

A famous study of performance was conducted in Chicago from 1924 to 1933 at a factory named the Hawthorne Works of the Western Electric Company. This study was originally designed to understand the effect of how different levels of illumination would impact worker performance (i.e., whether brighter light or less light made productivity go up or down). The common takeaway of the experiment was that the performance of participants was changed more so by the fact that they knew they were being studied, rather than by the actual factors being manipulated (illumination). This phenomenon was subsequently referred to as The Hawthorne Effect. There has been a lot of study and debate about the validity of this phenomenon, but it brings up an important consideration to think about when measuring productivity and service levels—and that is, the reliability of the data, since people know they are being measured.

A Personal Story about Measurement Bias

In the early 1990s I was giving a training workshop on Total Quality Management to front-line employees of an outsourcing division of Pitney Bowes Corporation that operated copy and mail centers within corporate clients' offices. As the employees were tasked with improving operations at various company sites, they were asked to keep careful track of the amount of jobs each day that were not done correctly and that had to be done over. Despite repeated explanation that the error tracking would not be used against them and would not be tied to their individual performance measures, the number of jobs that had to be done over was routinely under-reported by employees.

Except at one site.

At this one location the employees were more shrewd and they realized that *if the name of the game was improvement, then the more mistakes they had to start with, the more they would look like heroes when things got better!*

While most of the other teams were consistently shaving errors off their tracking reports and turning a blind eye to counting others, the members of this particular team were ruthless sticklers about what constituted a mistake, and they were vigorously logging them.

I guess there should be credit given for honesty and, as it turned out, this particular team was repeatedly pointed to and lavished with praise for what a great job they were doing, while the other teams looked on and realized they had shot themselves in the foot by trying to "game" the system.

The moral of the story:

Don't be afraid of admitting your existing poor performance up front—if you are committed to improving it in the future.

QUALITY METRICS

Measuring the qualitative aspects of your processes is something that was touched on in chapter 1. The question remains: How do you establish this balance and introduce it into your dashboard metrics?

Satisfaction surveys are a common way to keep a pulse on Quality of Service and these scores can be used to balance against traditional measures of cost, time, and inputs and outputs of a process. Though the process can be automated, this information must be gathered directly from the customer.

A fundamental concept of *HR Excellence* is the focus on improving and controlling overall processes to achieve business objectives. Rather than just trimming individual elements of your processes, the system as a whole is considered, taking into account that traditional trimming and streamlining may create short-term efficiencies at the expense of the overall business goals. For example, to address a reduced recruiting budget, an increase in spending on selection tools such as psychometric instruments may help to weed out candidates and result in lowered interviewing and travel expenses. The net impact on the budget may be neutral (or better) and will also result in improved hiring quality, increased productivity, and retention.

There are four key ways to measure the quality of your processes:

- **Effectiveness:** *How well the process meets customer needs.* Are the hiring managers getting the caliber of candidates to choose from that meets their needs?

- **Efficiency:** *The ability to be effective with the least amount of resources.* This might be measured through cost-per-hire or recruiting efficiency metrics. The critical factor in this is the ability to be effective and to still meet customer needs while keeping costs under control.

- **Experience:** *How being a part of the process feels for the customer(s).* An efficient and effective process that turns a blind eye to the experience of the customer may fall short (e.g., a poor experience for job applicants when applying online and having to spend unnecessary time with bureaucratic forms and procedures).

- **Adaptability:** *The ability to be both effective and efficient in the face of change.* This will determine the sustainability of your results over time, which will be where the true return on investment will come.

As noted previously, because qualitative aspects of HR were often not tracked in the past, different cost and time measures were often manipulated at the expense of the four above areas. Accomplishing a certain number of hires with a reduced budget does not translate into being more efficient if it was at the expense of service levels or candidate quality. True HR excellence will balance qualitative measures with quantitative ones—as well as build into the process the resilience to adapt to change and sustain these measures on an ongoing basis.

Just Check Here for "Excellent"—Gathering Meaningful Feedback and Satisfaction Scores

After visiting a local car dealership for some minor repairs, I received a letter from the service manager that explained I would be receiving a service questionnaire from the manufacturer that would ask me to rate the dealer's service. The letter showed a cut-away view of the form, pointing out where the "excellent" rating was on the page and impressing on me how important it was for their livelihood that I give the dealership high ratings. This always amuses me, since it is not the first time I have had this type of effort put into training me to give good ratings, rather than asking me how they can serve me better. Even medical staff at my HMO have gone to the trouble of pointing out where the high ratings are on their survey page (since I obviously can't read).

Is this really the pursuit of excellent customer service, or just the pursuit of excellent ratings? There is a difference.

The service manager (in his hand-signed letter) could have said something to the effect of:

> I pride myself on the consistent excellent ratings we receive from our customers. I encourage you to call me on my private line (555-1212) if you would like to share why you felt we did an excellent job, or, if you felt we did not deserve a rating of excellent so that I can improve how we operate. I would greatly appreciate your input.

Gathering Voice of the Customer data should be a continuous pursuit. Use it as a tool to constantly improve and not just to pat yourself on the back.

Final Thought: Use Metrics to Improve Your Game and Not Just to Keep Score

As stated earlier, metrics are about keeping score, and this book is about how to *improve your game.* You improve your game by breaking the score down into the sub-processes and transactions that make up the overall performance of your primary processes. To utilize a sports metaphor, if you only look at your total score and whether you won or lost, you have only generic directives like "get a higher score and win next time" or "keep winning." That isn't terribly helpful.

Instead, if you look at the number of times that you lost or missed an opportunity to score points, and identified *why* that was, or *what* you needed to do to increase your success in that area, then you're getting somewhere. You'll have a better idea of where you need to concentrate your efforts to score more points, and to be more successful when you get the ball, or at least not give points up to the other team! Then, as you improve at this by looking at where you had new success and figuring out how that can be replicated, you'll be moving closer to more success, or at least less failure, each time you have an opportunity with the ball.

In HR, we look at each customer transaction as the time when we each get the ball. What do you do? Score points for your team, or get penalties? In an HR transaction, what a "point" actually is can be more difficult to define, but when you look back at your responses to the earlier discussions about the Voice of the Customer (VOC) you should *have a better idea* about what success or failure looks like in the eyes of your customer.

To begin to bring the loop full circle, the next step is to start gathering additional data to help you understand what is driving your metrics by looking back to your Critical-to-Quality factors. The CTQs are what you need to look at more carefully and, if you've done a good job at identifying these, better measurement and subsequent management of them will translate into better overall performance.

In God we trust, all others bring data.

(W. Edwards Deming, American statistician, 1900–1993)

ANALYZE

With enough understanding of your process and your customers, you can now begin to look at the measurements and come up with some deeper analysis to help you craft improvements. This begins with understanding the cause-and-effect relationships between the input variables and the output or outcomes within your processes.

By utilizing graphical and statistical tools, you will be better able to understand patterns and trends that will lead you toward effective and sustainable improvements.

ANALYSIS TOOLS

CAUSAL ANALYSIS TOOLS

ANALYSIS TOOLS

If the only tool you have is a hammer,
everything starts to look like a nail.

(Abraham H. Maslow, psychologist, 1908–1970)

Now I will introduce you to a variety of tools to help you to analyze and understand the data that's been gathered. You may be familiar with some or all of these tools, but chances are they're not currently being used in your daily HR operations. I will be giving you a sampling of ways you might apply the tools, but this is not intended as a comprehensive list. As you look at different tools for analysis, it is important to note that some of the tools will help you understand the measurements you have gathered from your processes, while others will help you understand the cause-and-effect relationships in your processes. Both are of value as means to understand how to best drive your process results in the future.

Front Windshield vs. Rearview Mirror

The tools represented below will allow you to make sense of the data that has been gathered, and to analyze your processes so as to make sound business decisions. These tools are intended to help you understand what is happening in your processes so that you can *use the information that has been gathered to improve the future—and not just as a reporting mechanism to show what has taken place in the past.*

In other words, these tools should be used as decision-making tools for the future and not just as pretty charts and graphs demonstrating what you have already done.

It is the difference between driving a car and looking out the front windshield, instead of only looking in the rearview mirror.

Gap Analysis

As you utilize the graphical tools shown in this chapter, it is important to understand the difference between current process performance and customer requirements. This gap, if one exists, must be identified, as well as why it exists and how it can be reduced to meet customer requirements.

Equally important is the need to understand if there is a process capability limitation that inhibits performance. In essence, is the process *capable* of meeting customer-requirement levels? This can be a function of fluctuating demand and timing issues, or simply an indication of a process that is incapable of meeting normal customer requirements.

If there is a difference between current or historical process performance and what it is capable of, what is the cause? The identification of service gaps must take place in order to assess what can be controlled to improve the process by either closing, or reducing, the gap.

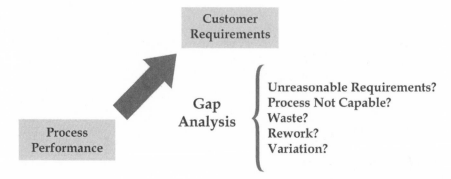

FIGURE 7-1

Tools to Understand Process Performance

1. Histograms and Bar Charts
2. Pareto Analysis
3. Flowcharts
4. Run Charts
5. Control Charts.

Histograms and Bar Charts

The histogram is a useful tool for breaking out process data into columns for determining frequencies of certain events or categories of data. These charts can help to show the most frequent causes of problems, the distribution of process data, or to provide other process improvement information.

The histogram will help you to understand the distribution or clustering of data. The histogram is best used for variables whose values are numerical and measured on an interval scale (meaning there is standard distance between each interval, such as dollars or days). It is used when dealing with large data sets, generally greater than 100 observations. A histogram can also help detect any unusual observations (outliers) or any gaps in the data.

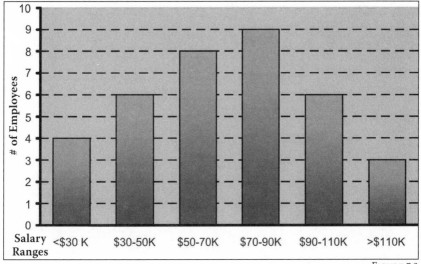

FIGURE 7-2

A histogram is generally shown as a bar chart. The natural order of the categories is maintained when performing a histogram. Note that a Pareto Chart (next page) sorts the categories from most common to least common.

Although histograms and bar graphs look very similar, histograms sort a single variable into *bins*. After identifying what each bin will represent (e.g., salaries in $10,000 increments), the data is placed in the appropriate bin. The number of units (salary increments) in each bin is then counted and that determines the height of the rectangle in the histogram for that bin.

Bar Chart—Average Salaries by Job Type

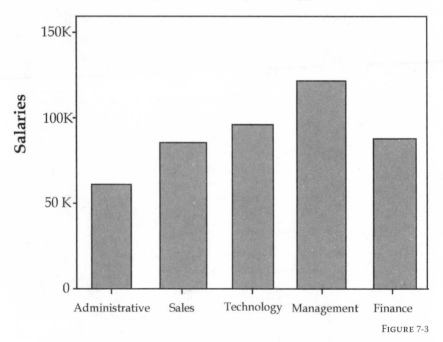

FIGURE 7-3

A bar chart compares a measurement (or several measurements) from different items. The main question a histogram answers is: "How many measurements are there in each of the classes (columns) of measurements?" The main question a bar graph answers is: "What is the measurement for each item?" Here are some examples:

Situation	Bar Graph or Histogram?	Question the tool is answering
We want to compare average salaries of different jobs.	Bar graph	What is the average salary for each job?
We want to compare the hiring source for hires made in January (employee referral, newspaper ad, job board, etc.).	Histogram	How many hires are attributed to each source?
We want to compare time to hire of ten different requisitions for different types of jobs.	Bar graph	How long did each requisition take to fill?
We want to compare the different times a requisition might take to fill and we want to sort them into 2-week increments (0–2 weeks, 2–4 weeks, 4–6 weeks, 6–8 weeks, etc.).	Histogram	How many requisitions fall into each two week time increment?

Pareto Chart

The Pareto Chart is a histogram that is ranked with the column that has the highest frequency to the left and the column with the smallest frequency to the right. What the Pareto Chart also adds is a percentage to the right side that will show you how the individual columns would stack up to equal 100%.

This is one of the simplest tools and yet it is the one deserving of the most attention. The concept of the vital few, also known as the 80/20 rule, was developed by an Italian mathematician named Pareto. The rule is that 80% of what happens is often influenced by 20% or less of the inputs. For example, 20% of your salespeople sell 80% of the products; 80% of your problems come from 20% of your managers. This rule is not perfect (none truly are) but it will help you to think about what to focus on. By grouping things together and stacking them in descending order you can visually see where to best focus your energies. Then you can begin the process of dividing-

and-conquering. Let's look at an example:

You have carefully tracked all of the employee insurance beneficiary forms that had to be resubmitted because of mistakes. You counted all the different reasons they had to be redone (defects or mistakes), grouped them, and ranked them in the chart below. Now you have an accurate idea of what you need to focus on in the future in order to reduce the number of mistakes.

Reasons Insurance Beneficiary Forms Were Rejected*

Lacked Complete Beneficiary Name and Information	5	31.25%
Lacked Beneficiary Payment %s	4	25%
Beneficiary Payment %s Did Not Equal 100%	3	18.75%
No Social Security or Employee ID #	2	12.5%
Not Signed	2	12.5%
Total	**16**	**100%**

The count for individual reasons are totaled (5 + 4 + 3 + 2 + 2 = 16) and then the % value for each reason is calculated by dividing the total number of each reason by the sum of all columns (5 ÷ 16 = .3125 or 31.25%).

Causes of Rejected Insurance Beneficiary Forms

Pareto Analysis

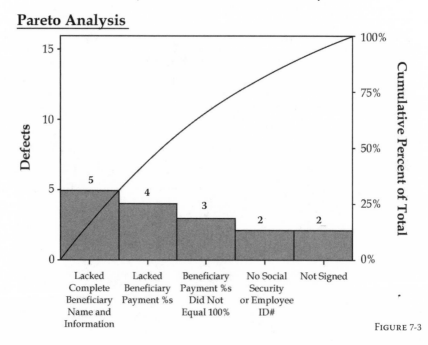

FIGURE 7-3

When you step back to take a more careful look at your biggest problem in this example (Lacked Complete Beneficiary Name and Information), you may come to understand that there may be several, or perhaps many, reasons for it. You can then use this same model to create another Pareto Analysis around the particular reason or reasons. Then supplied with this information, you will be able to discern the biggest contributing factors to the overall problem. If these are controllable, you can attack these first, and systematically work your way through toward improvement.

Flowcharts

In Chapter 5, I discussed the use of flowcharts and process maps to help you understand your processes better. Flowcharts can also be used as a tool to analyze your processes more deeply. Rather than looking just at the big picture, you can zoom in and focus on very specific tasks and the details of what happens in a process.

To help identify areas where a process might be streamlined, I will add a new symbol to the basic flowcharting shapes we discussed in chapter 6. The new shape represents delays that take place in the process. This could be when you are waiting for approval from a manager, or for some other reason that impedes the process from moving directly from one task to the next. In chapter 9, I will talk more about ways to improve processes, but here is an example of how you might identify delays and how a process might be realigned to save time.

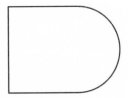

Delay Symbol

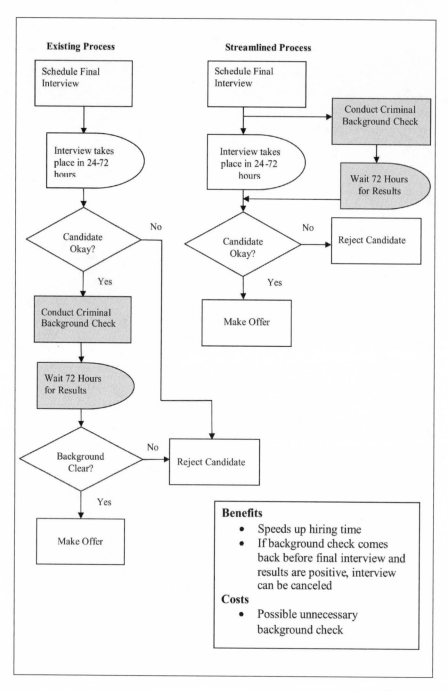

FIGURE 7-4

Run Charts

Both the run charts and the control charts (discussed in the next section) will help you examine data over time to spot trends and answer the question of, "Are we moving in the right direction?"

In the run chart below, the X (bottom line) represents a variable of time and the Y (vertical line) represents the value of the data. This can reveal simple trends that may happen based on business cycles whether they occur seasonally, monthly, annually, and so forth. See Figure 7-5.

Ideally, the run chart will demonstrate improvements as you continue to fine-tune your operations through *HR Excellence!*

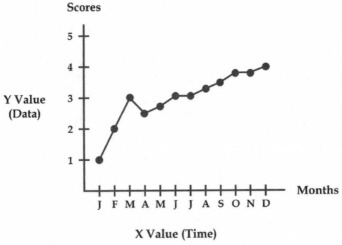

Average Satisfaction Scores from Training Attendees

FIGURE 7-5

Control Charts

Control charts are one of the more foreign tools for HR professionals, who normally are not used to thinking about their processes in terms of eliminating variation. Rather, most of us think primarily in terms of just reducing cost, time, and mistakes. (For a refresher on the importance of this issue, reread the discussion on reducing variation on page 24.)

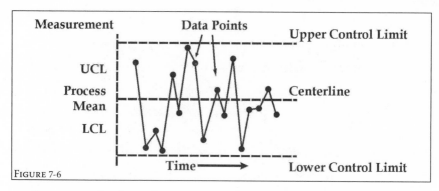

FIGURE 7-6

For example, how far can an HR call center transaction (call) be reduced without losing the human touch and making the caller feel like he or she is being hustled off the line? There is probably a minimum time to effectively establish rapport and gather enough information to answer the call effectively. That might make up the statistical Lower Control Limit.

The other end is the statistical Upper Control Limit and this is the longer length of calls. When data points go outside the upper limit, the question that arises is "why"? Again, you will not be looking for isolated data points or anomalies, but trends that tell you call lengths are rising and you need to look more carefully at the process to understand what is causing this.

The process of establishing and narrowing the control limits can then be improved by shifting them to a more desirable state of control. For example: taking days to fill and narrowing the control time to between 60 and 90 days; after that, the entire control time could be narrowed by 15 days and then shifted to between 45 and 60 days.

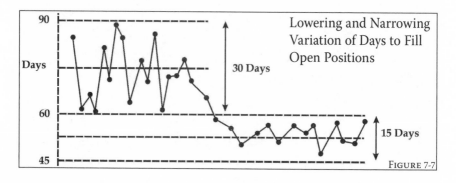

FIGURE 7-7

The Goal Post Analogy

A common teaching analogy to help people understand Lower and Upper Control Limits is to turn the chart on its side and to think about the Upper and Lower Limits as the two side polls of a football goal post. Getting between the two polls is the objective, and anything outside their bounds is not desirable.

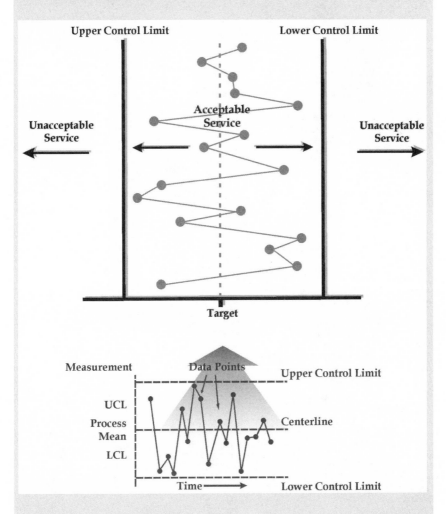

FIGURE 7-8

Causal Analysis Tools

The cause ceasing, the effect ceases also.

(Edward Coke, English businessman, *1552–1634*)

Managing HR by Facts

WHILE speaking with HR professionals over the years about cause-and-effect and controlling variables in HR, I've noticed that many people resist the notion that clear cause-and-effect can be tied to many things in HR. The common thought is that there are just too many variables outside the control of the HR professional. Although that may be true in part, my point is that more HR decisions should be based on facts and due diligence than presently occurs. Think of it as a linear scale: management by guesswork on one end and strict scientific management on the other. The goal is to move further along the scale and further away from guesswork to managing more by facts.

Management by Guesswork　　　　　　**Management by Facts**

⟶

Even as we refine the use of analytic tools and incorporate it more into HR operations, there is still an element of trial and error that will continue to take place. That's okay. The goal is to make better, more informed decisions that are based on quality data.

The following three tools will help you understand the root causes and relationship between variables in your processes:

1. Scatter Plots
2. Cause-and-Effect Diagrams
3. Five "Whys" Analysis.

Scatter Plots

Scatter plots show us whether there is a correlation between two variables:

- X variable on the bottom, which increases in value from left to right, and
- Y variable, which increases in value from the bottom to the top.

By plotting the individual data points you can visually represent the overall data and identify any correlation between the two variables.

There may be a strong correlation between the two variables, in which case a line can be drawn that generally represents the trend. If there is no correlation, the data points will be spread out without showing any specific trend. This visual representation will allow you to take a column of data and create the scatter plot next to it, to show if any trend exists.

x	y
2	60
6	75
8	90
3	62
5	65
7	85
1	40
4	72
9	90

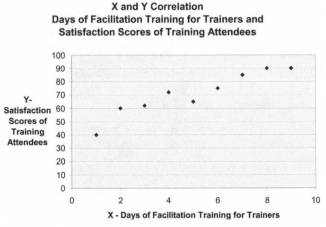

FIGURE 8-1

In this case, there is a strong, positive correlation. Now that you know this, you can manipulate one variable, and better predict the result of the other. This scatter plot approach will allow you to manipulate your process results by viewing the relationship between variables and to know which levers to pull to drive your HR process results.

Types of Correlation

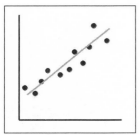 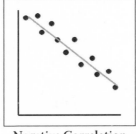 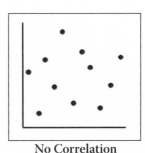

| Positive Correlation | Negative Correlation | No Correlation |

FIGURE 8-2

Cause-and-Effect or Fishbone Diagrams

The cause-and-effect diagram is also known as a fishbone diagram (and sometimes as an Ishigawa diagram *). This chart facilitates understanding the root causes of different effects.

The "head of the fish" is the topic or effect that is being analyzed. Off the spine of the fish there are four or more major bones that represent major causes; minor causes are then branched off from there.

In a service environment such as HR, there are four key branches to explore. They normally fall under the four P's:

Place	How does our technology, location, or physical environment affect . . . ?
Procedure	What procedures are causing . . . ?
People	How do our people influence . . . ?
Policies	What regulations or internal policies affect . . . ?

---

* Named after its creator, Kaoru Ishikawa, a Japanese consultant and leader in the scientific analysis of causes in industrial processes.

There may be other categories and this is okay; the diagram is meant to create understanding and is not of strict form. Lines may be added to represent additional major causes. As you fill in your cause-and-effect diagram you may need to take a closer look at certain causes. The next tool, the Five "Whys," may be needed to help you complete this diagram.

FIGURE 8-3

Five "Whys": Figuring Out Root Causes

In my role of analyzing problems in organizations, I am proud to point out that as a child one of my favorite questions was "Why?" ("Why does the Teflon® stick to the pan, Mom?") In root cause analysis, asking *why* is exactly what we all must do. The process can normally be accomplished in a series of five rounds or less and is, therefore, called the Five "Whys."

This process is simple to do and requires no software, statistics, or other training. The only thing necessary is an understanding of the issue being worked on.

Five "Whys" Example

Problem: Recruiting time-to-fill periods are longer than desired.

1) Why? Managers aren't getting back to recruiters in a timely manner with feedback on resumes.

2) Why? Initial resumes the managers saw were not good fits, and they became apathetic and assumed future resumes would be another waste of time.

3) Why? Initial screening of resumes by recruiters was not effective.

4) Why? Requirements from the manager were not clear.

5) Why? Recruiters needed to spend more time identifying screening requirements before commencing the search.

It is interesting to note that the answer to "Why are recruiting times-to-fill periods longer than expected?" would result in an answer of "Need to spend more time" *doing* something in the HR process!

Quick Tips on Utilizing the Five "Whys"

- This exercise is followed until the root causes are identified and may involve more than five "whys" (or perhaps fewer).
- There may be several answers for each level of "why" questions, and each of these may have a series of different answers that follow after those. As a result, the answers may branch off at one or all levels and identify many "why" questions, and produce various root causes.
- Answering any level "why" question may need more investigation and may require finding out answers before proceeding. In our Five "Whys" example above, level 2 would probably have been answered by talking to the managers and trying to get their honest feedback. You might have a hypothesis, but it needs to be verified before proceeding—

else wise it will possibly result in following a wrong path of "whys" and coming to an erroneous root cause.

- Always keep asking what the root cause is, but stop at a reasonable point where a solution can be *implemented* that fixes the problem. For instance, in our example, the final "why" was shaped into more of a solution rather than an answer leading into a question of "Why aren't recruiters spending enough time identifying screening requirements?" This could go on indefinitely in some cases and needs to be balanced with finding the most efficient and logical solution.

Advanced Tools in Appendix A

There are other tools that can be used in your quest for HR excellence, but these may be unnecessary when utilizing what you already know to drive some initial improvements. Therefore, I have selected a few additional advanced tools that can be found in Appendix A.

These tools are used even less frequently in HR than those covered in this chapter, but they can be incredibly valuable in analysis, decision making, and in helping you manage by facts.

It is important to note that, though these tools may take a little more effort to understand and learn, they can bring more definitive answers to strategic decisions that you may need to make. Take the time to read through them to give yourself a sense of what is available to improve operations.

Though you may not utilize them today, you may find that you need them in the future.

  KEY THOUGHT

Remember: Using the right tool effectively is more important than how many tools you have.

IMPROVE

Now that you have taken the time to understand your processes, and to measure and analyze them, you should have a reasonable amount of information with which to diagnose and move toward prescribing a solution. This may involve streamlining, or it may take the form of automating through HR technology, or it may mean outsourcing part or all of the process.

PROCESS IMPROVEMENT

HR TECHNOLOGY

OUTSOURCING

CHANGE MANAGEMENT

> Define >> Measure >> Analyze >> Improve >> Control >

Process Improvement

If you do what you've always done,
you'll get what you've always gotten.

(Tony Robbins, author and speaker)

Now that you have gathered enough data to help you understand your processes better, it's time to figure out how to improve them! There are many different possible approaches and I will cover some things for you to keep in mind, and also provide an easy-to-remember model for creating improvements which is called the E-S-C-A-P-E Method.

Incremental vs. Breakthrough Improvement

There are different approaches to improving a process and they can be separated into two categories: incremental and breakthrough. *Incremental* process improvement takes an existing process and tries to make adjustments to it while keeping the basic process intact. *Breakthrough* process improvement is a more drastic approach that scraps the existing process and creates a new process from scratch, based on customer requirements. This is the difference between adjusting what you have currently, versus scrapping everything and starting with a clean sheet of paper.

However, there are pros and cons to each approach.

While incremental improvement is most common, it may not yield the level of results that a breakthrough improvement effort might provide. A breakthrough improvement may carry greater risks though, since the new process may have additional variables that were not previously present and explored.

Mistake Proofing

Sometimes fixing a process simply means eliminating the things that keep going wrong. This may not mean that the whole process needs to be redesigned, but rather that something must be done to eliminate the defects and errors in a process. The Japanese call this Poke Yoke (pronounced po-kay yo-kay), which means *mistake proofing*.

Mistake proofing strives to put safety catches into a process to stop mistakes from happening. For example, changing the color of the text in certain areas of an employment offer letter where mistakes commonly happen can help reduce errors. By changing the colors of the text in the word-processing template, it forces the person using the template to look more carefully at those sections and to make those parts stand out from the rest of the text. When the user fills in required information, they are able to quickly focus on the critical parts where mistakes happen and must consciously change the color of these sections back to black.

The "E-S-C-A-P-E" Approach
to Improving a Process

As you think about how to improve your process, here is a simple and easy way to remember to look at your processes. The acronym E-S-C-A-P-E outlines steps that you can take when looking critically at individual tasks or an entire process:

- **E**liminate
- **S**implify

- Combine
- Automate
- Parallel Path
- Empower

Eliminate

What can you get rid of? It can be that simple. What tasks can simply go away? There are:

- Historical reports you've created that nobody really reads but you still keep creating them.

- Forms that are filled out and filed and never referenced again.

- "Required" signatures that are really unnecessary.

- Steps in the process that the customer doesn't care about, know about, or will ever miss.

If possible, eliminate them!

Simplify

If a task cannot be eliminated, can it somehow be simplified? How can the work be reduced, but still accomplish the goal of the task? For example, email has replaced a lot of unnecessary paper reports and communications, which has cut down dramatically on the cost of printing and physically distributing information. Is there a next step?

How about:

- Making the information available on demand?
- Putting it in a shared folder for access when needed, rather than flooding everyone's email inbox?
- Slimming down the report information so it is easier to read (dashboard metrics with drill down information)?

Combine

By combining tasks, you may utilize a combination of simplifying and eliminating tasks. This can mean integrating tasks that were previously done as separate steps or adjusting the timing of when the steps are done. In combining tasks, the issue of who does a particular task can also be examined. Rather than having one person do one thing and then moving the task to the next person, multiple tasks can be done by the same person to save on movement between people, departments, etc.

This may also fall under the *Empower* component, mentioned later.

Automate

In the next chapter, I will discuss the use of technology in HR in more detail. The attempt to automate manual processes is a strong option for improving HR processes, but often automation has already been explored by HR departments and some improvements may have already been introduced. What else can be automated, though? Where does the automation start and stop? Ask yourself if the scope of automation in a process can be extended (e.g., getting rid of the paper form that still gets printed out and signed for internal purposes at the end of an otherwise automated and paperless process).

Parallel Steps

Let's abandon our linear thinking here for a moment and question the sequence of activities. We need to look at predecessors (what happens or needs to happen before a task) and consider how critical it is that certain activities follow another. Now a single person can only do one task at a time, but as tasks get split up, they can enter the process at, perhaps, an earlier time or a later time depending on their interdependence with other tasks and available resources.

What do I mean by interdependence and predecessors? I suggest looking at the task like a process in the SIPOC exercise previously discussed in chapter 2, and then asking two key questions:

- What does this task produce?
- What are the inputs required to do this task?

If the inputs that are required are dependent on the task right before it, then the task cannot be started until the preceding task is finished. If that isn't the case, then the task can be done earlier, in parallel with other tasks.

The questions that need to be asked then are:

- Will additional waste be created by doing a task earlier or in a different sequence?
- And, most importantly, will the time savings outweigh any additional costs or waste that is produced?

See the example in chapter 7 that demonstrates how moving tasks in parallel can improve a process.

Empower

A lack of empowerment is at the root of much process inefficiency. Empowerment may involve removing extra steps taking place in a process which often cause delays. These steps might include the need to inspect the work of others. This may be due to errors that have historically taken place and a step was added to catch the errors. Instead of adding steps for checking the work of others, if you work on fixing the problems (input factors) that cause the errors in the first place, you can eliminate or reduce this need for oversight.

The step of requiring a signature in a process is a sure sign of something to examine when it comes to empowerment. I often ask clients, "How often do you *not* sign off on these things?" The answer is normally rarely or never. The good news is that the process is working. However, the extra signature is probably an unnecessary step. Why have it? Get rid of that step. Make your requirements clear, and empower whoever needs to be empowered to streamline the process without compromising quality.

Benchmarking: A Tool for Process Improvement

Benchmarking was a popular term used during the '90s, when re-engineering was a common topic. Benchmarking is still a great tool for improvement, but I find the term normally comes up in HR in the context of metrics and performance measurement.

Let's look more closely at the term, and examine how benchmarking can be used as an effective tool for improvement in HR.

Here is a standard definition of benchmarking:

> *Benchmarking: An improvement process in which a company measures its performance against that of best-in-class companies, determines how those companies achieved their performance levels and uses the information to improve its own performance. The subjects that can be benchmarked include strategies, operations, processes and procedures.* (ASQ Quality Glossary)

Benchmarking helps bring additional information into the discussion of the improvement of operations. It allows an external perspective, and often shows alternate ways of looking at and approaching a process.

There are many great benefits that can be gleaned from the process of benchmarking and it can definitely prompt new ways of looking at a problem. I have a few pet peeves that I will point out, which frame some key issues about how benchmarking often isn't, but can be, utilized more effectively.

For additional resources on benchmarking, see the Online Resource Center.

My Pet Peeves

(and Three Keys to Better Benchmarking)

Follow the Whole Benchmarking Model

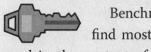 Benchmarking is a tool that I find most HR practitioners have used in the context of *just comparing metrics with other organizations* (e.g., cost-per-hire, benefits costs per employee, turnover, etc.). That is great . . . but it is only part of the process in doing effective benchmarking. For example, finding out what the turnover rate at a great company is can be a motivating target, but it is only half of the battle. It misses the critical step in the definition given above of *"determine how those companies achieved their performance levels,"* meaning, you need to figure out how they did it! Armed with this, you can use the information to help you improve your own processes.

Model the Right Organizations

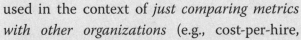 Another big issue I have with the use of benchmarking is the indiscriminate selection of organizations to model. Benchmarking is supposed to be the study and emulation of best-in-class companies, but all too often I find most organizations just studying convenient and easy-to-reach organizations. While some outside information is useful compared to none, the focus really should be on identifying and copying from the best. This may take some doing, but the efforts are well worth it.

Keep Perspective and Don't Just Imitate

While benchmarking is a useful process for gathering information and getting ideas, it must in no way be utilized as a primary method for creating improvements in your operation. The reason is that all too often *the customers that best-in-class company is serving are not your customers, and other variables may effect your organization's performance.*

Therefore, you cannot force process changes into your environment and expect that, just because they worked across the street, they will work for your organization. Use benchmarking to gather ideas and not just to find another organization's processes to mimic.

10

HR Technology

The first rule of any technology used in a business is that automation applied to an efficient operation will magnify the efficiency. The second is that automation applied to an inefficient operation will magnify the inefficiency.

(Bill Gates, founder, Microsoft Corporation)

T HE introduction of database software and Internet-based products and services have added tremendous value to the HR industry and the profession in general, yet there has been a significant part of the "e-HR" promise that has remained elusive and unfulfilled. But rather than reviewing the merits of HR technology, or rehashing the realities of what is viable and what's not, I will make the assertion that the automation and streamlining of certain HR operations through the use of technology is desirable, even required, to survive in today's global economy. To begin to frame this discussion, let's consider these key points:

- The reporting and data gathering capabilities of HR technology are a critical part of the value proposition and these need to be capitalized on to make this information timely, actionable, and useful for improving HR operations.
- If the implementation of HR technology does not *innovate while creating efficiencies,* it will simply automate and speed up *bad* processes.
- A great deal of the functionalities in HR technology go unused due to a lack of training, too many user-adoption issues, and overall ineffective utilization of what is available.

The following diagram addresses two of the key issues that technology brings to the table in HR: actionable information and process efficiency.

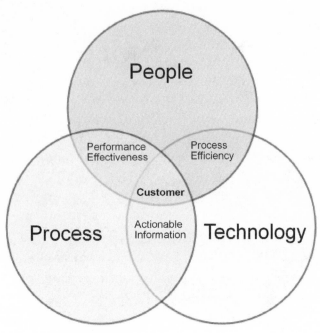

FIGURE 10-1

Actionable Information

The ability to gather information for strategic use is a key aspect of HR technology. Though I have spoken about metrics in chapter 6, an important aspect of technology is using it for gathering data about your processes. Therefore, it is important to discuss it again within the context of improving the value of your HR technology. In short, HR technology can help you better understand how long things take, and how many transactions you're doing, as well as a wealth of data that will allow you to fine-tune your processes and better allocate resources.

Real-time availability of data through reporting is a tremendous aid in enabling you to improve the efficiency of your HR operations. Rather than gathering historical data at the end of the year, quarter, or month, information can instead be retrieved and acted upon that week, day, or even down to the moment. This data can also be gathered with negligible impact on staff resources because information can be gathered without asking staff members to stop what they're doing to report on their activities. The discreet nature of this type of data gathering reduces the possibility of biased information (e.g., staff fabricating their reports to make their productivity look better than it is).

Technology can be a significant aid in gathering actionable information which can lead to improvements. The following table summarizes some of the key benefits of utilizing technology to gather better data:

Benefit of Technology	Typical Problem Addressed
Real-time	There is a lag in the time the data was gathered and it may not reflect the current state of "things."
Inexpensive	Gathering the data may be cost prohibitive in a manual process.
Unbiased	Manually gathered data may be biased in that it is not gathered in a strict manner (selective memory), or it may be intentionally slanted by the data gatherer to omit negative information or to accentuate positive information.
Scalable	If a sample is taken, the data may not be representative of the greater population.

Process Efficiency

Automation has been a key aspect of improving efficiency in all areas of business. Because of the traditionally non-technical nature of HR, it has been slow in adopting technology to replace what were formerly paper-based processes. There are many reasons for this, and different organizations are at various stages of this movement toward a *paperless process.*

Moving toward the elimination of paper serves several needs from addressing the cost and effort of storage and retrieval of data, to the use of data in other systems. A case for this need not be made, but an enormous volume of manual, paper-based aspects of HR administrative processes continues to diminish efficiency and productivity. Often a process gets automated up to a certain point, but not far enough. Getting manual signatures for non-contractual documents is a good example. A form is printed that needs authorization and instead of implementing electronic signature systems to save time and paper, hard-copy approval is required to take place on paper so that executives can sign a requisition or formalize an agreement.

The signing of documents such as performance reviews carries a psychological commitment, as well as being a legal document that may be referenced in a wrongful termination lawsuit. There are many other examples where manual signatures still take place for approvals that are deemed important in the organization, but in many cases the need for a paper signature is not justifiable.

While I am not a lawyer, and will therefore refrain from giving advice on which documents must remain paper-based and which should not, this is an area where improvement opportunities exist and you should carefully look at all instances where signatures are required, or where paper-based HR files are kept.

In addition to the issue of efficiency, there is another key issue in this discussion which I will take up next.

Use Technology to Innovate and *Not Just to Automate*

In the past decade, transactional HR (administrative services) has undergone a dramatic evolution through the use of database technology and the Internet. Most organizations have reacted by adopting technology to replace labor-intensive services, but many have fallen short at truly innovating how they operate.

Like many things in business and life, we often continue to do things out of habit or become reactive by implementing quick-fixes that don't really address our problems. We fail to ask ourselves what the core problems are and how we should address and improve them.

To illustrate this point, what follows is an interesting piece of history.

Is Your HR Process Like the Typewriter?*

The standard computer keyboard uses the same layout from the original typewriter design that has been around for about 130 years. Some of you probably were taught this famous QWERTY design in high school typing class (or "keyboarding" class for those more recent graduates). If this was how you were taught, you would assume that the keyboard layout was designed for maximum efficiency. This design probably came from extensive engineering, testing, and refinement, right?

Actually, no, it did not. Historical accounts tell us that the current design was not the result of it being the most efficient layout. Some say it was an intentional scrambling of the keyboard to *slow down* the typist because the mechanical parts could not keep up and would otherwise jam. Other accounts put the design as a clever marketing ploy by Remington (the company that first created the typewriter) so that their salesmen could quickly punch out the letters "type write" in demonstrations and all of those letters appear in the top row of the QWERTY design.

---

* Adapted from original article by Scott Weston first published 6/3/2003 on the "Electronic Recruiting Exchange" www.erexchange.com.

Whatever happened, improvements to the original QWERTY design always met with resistance, despite countless studies, alternate designs, and improvements. The U.S. Navy even did studies in the 1940s and tested other layouts that could increase typing speeds. Changes never took place, though, since the cost to retrain the existing staff and change equipment seemed too daunting.

The point is that the keyboard design we still use today is not necessarily the most efficient—yet it has survived through generations of technical evolutions, including electronic typewriters and modern computer keyboards. And, all these years later, with all new workers and all new equipment, millions of people are still typing slower than they could.

With this in mind, now may be a good time to take the time to review and analyze your HR processes and your use of HR technology and ask some tough questions about the true benefits and return on investment you are experiencing, and how these might be improved.

 KEY THOUGHT *Carefully question processes that you are automating. Make sure you are innovating at the same time as automating and not perpetuating inefficiency—or making a bad process faster.*

Five Quick Tips to Improve Your Use of HR Technology

HR technology is more robust than many users realize. Often, it is a matter of just not taking the time to set up the features that can most benefit their operations. I have spoken with many sales reps who tell stories of customers already in the process of shopping for new technology, maybe a new HRIS, claiming that their system "isn't suiting their needs" without having a true understanding of its capabilities.

This may be the result of the system never being properly set up or fully utilized from the start. It also occurs when there are staff changes and the incoming users end up learning just enough of the system to get by, but never really become versed in the system's true capabilities. The following five tips can help you more effectively utilize your existing technology to achieve greater efficiency.

#1 Elect a Power User

Instead of having everyone go through training again or sit down and read the manual, elect a "power user." This person will be in charge of doing research on behalf of the team and distilling the information into tips and suggestions for training.

This power user may be the department manager or one of your more technical users, but it must be someone who is comfortable with technology and willing to share what she knows. Chances are there is a staff person who is more adept at the system, a person people already gravitate to for help. Make this person your team's official power user, then ask the power user to spend an hour or two and come up with the five best tips for the team to improve their use of the system.

#2 Tap Other Resources in Your Organization

Check with your training and IT departments for assistance. You may be surprised at the wealth of knowledge they can offer in areas such as creating reports and other common database issues. Many report writing tools are similar and someone adept at report creation in another software package may be able to significantly reduce the learning curve in your package.

3 Break Training Down into Smaller Bites

One of the main problems with training for any product or service is information overload. To combat this, identify the highest leveraged activities first, instead of trying to learn or relearn the whole system. By tackling things in smaller sections or breaking the information down into a series of tips and learning these over time, there is more chance that the information will be adopted into use.

For example, each week assign a section of the manual or part of the system to a different member of your team and ask that person to master it and present a 10- to 15-minute summary at your weekly meeting, or to come up with a tip for the week. This will encourage proficiency across your team, and it will lighten the load of one user having to act as the help desk for your entire department.

#4 Talk to Your Vendors

Look to your vendors as partners and don't be afraid to ask them for help. This seems obvious, but I have found many vendors saddened and often shaking their heads at how under-utilized their products and services normally are.

If you have a good relationship with your sales representative, start there and ask if he can give you suggestions. Most vendors offer retraining or advanced training. This may be at a price, though, so make it clear that you may want to exhaust other options before you go that route.

Also consider putting in a call to the implementation consultant who set up your system, or the trainer you originally worked with. Let her know you feel you may not be making full use of the system and ask if she can offer some suggestions.

Most vendors are happy to do a certain amount of this without a charge as a service to their customers—since it also often identifies issues and opens the door to customization, add-on projects, or additional training revenues.

Be clear about your intentions and respectful of your vendor's time when asking for help. Make the effort on your own to first read the manuals and to use other information already available to you.

5 Utilize Online Forums and User Groups

Remember, you are not the only organization using any particular type of HR technology. There are online forums and user groups that you can join to find answers to Frequently Asked Questions and "fixes" that other organizations have come up with for common problems. This is also a great place to find information before purchasing a new system, or on interfacing with other applications and systems such as payroll, time and attendance, or other technology that may not be supported by your vendor as part of its "official" technical support.

Employee Self-Service and Manager Self-Service

Employee Self-Service with Light Ice:
Some Additional Thoughts on HR Technology

The use of online forms and automated workflow to empower employees and managers is respectively referred to as Employee Self-Service (ESS) and Manager Self-Service (MSS). Both are becoming increasingly considered as viable innovations to improve HR processes. Despite this, there is some question regarding the net benefits of self-service to organizations. To frame this discussion, I would like to share a business example that is outside of HR.

In the fast-food industry, McDonald's restaurant installed beverage dispensing machines that saved labor costs by dispensing the proper amount of a drink at the push of a button and not requiring counter staff to stand there while the cup filled. But often customers still had requests for light ice, or the cups needed to be filled a little bit more when the pre-measured level didn't come quite to the top. Other fast-food restaurants, on the other hand, looked at the costs of labor and compared that to the costs of the syrup and water that made up the beverages and realized that by giving the customers the ability to fill the drinks themselves and to give themselves refills, this ultimately resulted in better profits and happier customers.

There is a similar logic chain in HR which is that by off-loading certain administrative tasks to the employees themselves, HR expenses can be reduced. However, this isn't necessarily the case because, although the HR expenses might be reduced, overall organizational labor expenses might not be. In the fast-foot example, the customers filling their own drinks did not work for the restaurants—while HR's customers (employees and managers) work for the organization.

Question: Do you track what time of day your employees use different self-service options? Have you quantified this into cost of labor (if it is during business hours) and then factored this into your ROI?

To be clear, Employee Self-Service and Manager Self-Service can be wonderful improvements to your HR processes, but, when integrating them into your HR operations and in gauging their ROI, make sure you consider factors such as: the cost of *all* labor, the initial learning curve for the user, and in what ways this process can still be improved. An example of possible improvements might be to integrate collaborative technology solutions which allow the remote sharing of screens so that HR personnel can offer assistance in a real-time and virtual manner, much like technical support is offered now in other areas.

SUCCESSFUL OUTSOURCING

Like marriage, outsourcing is much easier to consummate
than it is to terminate, and recover from, if done poorly.

(Maurice F. Greaver II, author, *Strategic Outsourcing*)

I N your quest for HR excellence, outsourcing can be a key tool in the process-management efforts by bringing in critical outside resources to effectively serve your customers. Keep in mind, however, that outsourcing is not a quick-fix for deeper departmental or organizational problems and that too many organizations jump into outsourcing without effective strategic reasons or due diligence. The end result is often a less than optimal solution, or one that ends up being unsatisfactory and fails to create cost savings and/or service improvements. This chapter will cover what I believe to be some of the key aspects to consider if you want to outsource effectively.

Why Outsource?

Outsourcing in HR has actually been around for a long time—indeed, the use of third-party recruiters and payroll services have been a part of HR operations for many years. So, while the trend in outsourcing continues to rise, it is not a new concept for HR. Because of its increased use, though, outsourcing comes under more scrutiny and the question "why outsource?" looms.

While cost-cutting is often an initial driver and continues to be a strong element, the trend is to outsource for more strategic reasons that include, but are not limited to:

- Reducing operating costs and freeing up cash for capital to be used more effectively

- Improving HR service levels

- Allowing internal HR staff to focus on strategic issues

- Accessing additional talent, knowledge, and technology.

Therefore, the measurable cost savings are only one aspect of an HR outsourcing strategy. Improving HR's overall efficiency and effectiveness is also a key driver. And there is a focus on the overall qualitative aspects of its operations and service contribution that include the more core activities of recruiting, training, development, performance management, and retention, which are seen as more strategic HR activities as compared to some of the more transactional roles that HR plays in areas such as benefits enrollment, payroll processing, etc.

Certain services have also traditionally been outsourced by companies in an effort to manage risks by enlisting a third party to deal with delicate areas in employee relations. Some of these include: outplacement services, employee assistance programs (EAPs), COBRA administration, and defined benefit and pension plans. Another outsourced service is the use of external recruiting services (third-party executive search firms), who may be raiding competitors, suppliers, or even customers for talent, and the organization hiring them wants to have a layer between itself and its association with these activities. Such moves to outsource are driven by a desire to avoid potential lawsuits, to elicit third-party objectivity, or simply to reduce the discomfort in handling these tasks directly (e.g., outplacement services).

What to Outsource

A key reason to outsource is so that you can focus more attention on your core HR activities. But because of HR's *people element*, HR is a difficult area for some organizations to separate even partially from what is perceived as its core activities. If your organization is in the business of selling cars, providing financial services, or drilling for oil, then most if not all of your HR activities are really not core activities. The question arises more often than not, "What is sensible to let out of your control?"

Deciding which HR activities to keep in-house and which to outsource can be difficult. When looking at your list of HR activities and processes, focus first on the two ends of the scale, meaning those activities you absolutely do not wish to let go of because they are too critical to the organization and, on the other end, those activities that you would like to off-load, or are simply indifferent to. Placing these at both ends, you'll be able to fill in this scale and gain an understanding of what the gray areas of activities are (those that you may be on the fence about). Once there is a semblance of order, you can then rank activities to prioritize and refine this list even further. This analysis should give you an idea of where to begin an outsourcing strategy. Items that do not fall clearly at either end of the scale should be considered carefully, looking at factors such as:

- **Control:** Is this something you are willing to let out of your control?

- **Resources:** Are the resources available to accomplish this?

- **Cultural Issues:** Would outsourcing meet heavy internal resistance for some reason?

- **Service Levels:** Can future levels of service be maintained, even in the face of fluctuating demand levels?

- **The Economics of Outsourcing:** Does it make economic sense to outsource this activity?

Specific Voice of the Customer Questions on Outsourcing

It may be prudent to gather Voice of the Customer information again as you go down the path of exploring outsourcing as an improvement to your HR operations. Specific questions such as the following can be asked to help frame attitudes about outsourcing:

1. What HR activities are considered to be strategic? Why?

2. What HR activities might a vendor do better? Why?

3. What HR activities would you like to see outsourced? Why?

4. What HR activities would you be uncomfortable having outsourced? Why?

The Keys to HR Outsourcing

In order to effectively outsource, HR professionals must:

1. Understand their internal and external processes enough to have clear and reasonable requirements.

2. Carefully monitor their total outsourcing costs and return on investment.

3. Allocate sufficient resources to manage the outsourcing relationship effectively.

4. Perform due diligence in selecting an outsourcing supplier and constructing a partnership.

5. Be prepared for the outsourcing arrangement to end.

HR Outsourcing Key #1:

Understand Your Internal and External Processes Enough to Have Clear and Reasonable Requirements

Identifying what is to be outsourced is a critical activity. Going back to our SIPOC and process maps (chapters 2 and 6), a detailed statement of work must be a key part of the outsourcing agreement. The customer must be able to articulate in clear terms exactly what needs to be done and where responsibility for deliverables rests between the customer and vendor. There is often a misguided notion that a very dysfunctional HR process can be outsourced and, by doing so, it will be fixed. This can be a recipe for disaster.

You Cannot Outsource a Mess, or Something You Do Not Understand, and Expect Outsourcing to be Successful

It is incumbent upon the customer to have a clear understanding of what it needs and expects of the vendor. That is not to say that the vendor cannot be helpful in guiding clients through this process and helping them understand what they don't. This is especially true in areas of complex regulations, where subject matter expertise is one of the key driving forces that the organization is looking to a vendor to help manage.

The following are some of the aspects that need to be covered as you put together the outsourcing strategy created for the outsourcing project:

- Objectives for outsourcing
- Services to be offered
- Links between the outsourced process and the organization's core focus
- The relationship of the outsourcing process to the organization's strategy

- Environmental and strategic issues that are prompting outsourcing

- Duration, if there is one, of the outsourcing strategy

- Risks involved, both of outsourcing and of not outsourcing.

These bring up questions that need to be answered and decisions that will have to be made about how you are going to go about, and what you want to accomplish through, outsourcing. While not necessary, it can be formalized in a written outsourcing plan that lays out the strategy and goals for the outsourcing project. It can be done as a Project Charter similar to what was discussed in chapter 4. Just as I made the case for creating a Project Charter before you start a project, taking time to strategize before diving into outsourcing can also help this process immensely.

Sacred Cows

As you look at your customer requirements, it is critical to look at every step in a process and determine whether or not it is truly necessary (as defined by those customer requirements). Bundling in *ideal wish-list* requirements with your needed requirements may shift how the outsourcing supplier provides you service, and this may substantially affect the pricing structure. An example might be submitting requests for temporary labor electronically, instead of always talking to an account manager. While the personal interaction is nice, labor is expensive, and if there are not specific needs that are most efficiently handled directly with an account manager, maybe this is an aspect of the outsourcing service for which you are unnecessarily paying extra.

This is a time to ask for counsel from your outsourcing provider, and to elicit recommendations for the most efficient solution.

Tapping into Vendor Knowledge

Understanding the cost of your current activities is critical when commencing the exploration of outsourcing. Vendors can help by providing industry benchmarks of costs. While decisions should not necessarily be made solely on the numbers that you receive from vendors, don't pass up the opportunity to gather this vital data. Realize that part of the value vendors provide is that they often have a better understanding of the market then you do.

Tapping into this domain expertise from vendors is one of the key reasons many organizations outsource. Ask your vendors if they can provide you with third-party data that will help benchmark HR operational costs. This can save a lot of time and energy, as well as money, on your part as you clarify costs. You also have to take this with some skepticism because, if there were two conflicting industry studies, you can expect you will be shown the one most favorable to a particular vendor's business case.

I generally find that the vendors that are most forthcoming with this data tend to be those that have the most solid business models, competitive pricing, and a pulse on the HR marketplace—meaning they're constantly keeping abreast of current developments and economic trends in their industry.

HR Outsourcing Key #2:

Carefully Monitor Your Total Outsourcing Costs and Return on Investment (ROI)

In order to properly evaluate the cost/benefit aspect of outsourcing, it is necessary to have a thorough understanding of current costs. As you look at putting true costs on processes to be outsourced, both direct and indirect costs need to be factored in. The cost of contract administration must also be included. Budgeted costs are not necessarily good indicators of the cost of a process, so avoid budget numbers in your comparison of outsourcing costs even though these numbers are readily available.

Outsourcing Has to be Structured to Make Financial Sense

Saving money is one of the key reasons organizations outsource. Even though there may be additional reasons, outsourcing just plain has to make financial sense. Depending on the levels of investment that have already taken place in HR, outsourcing may or may not make sense. While many of these investments may be sunk* or fixed** costs, it is important to consider any balance sheet implications that they might have in the future. Existing investments in major HR technology are a good example.

How the contract is structured in terms of price is a critical area to consider. You must take into account fluctuations in transactions that may take place seasonally, or are tied to growth in your business (sudden or steady organic growth). And, what if your business declines and the need for the outsourcing services is diminished? Is there some threshold or trigger that will allow the contract to be adjusted?

The key is to take as much of the gamble out of a contract as possible. This might be accomplished by having a check-in after six months or a year to assess and/or to realign objectives. This check-in and adjustment may not initially be offered by the outsourcer and it is something you will probably have to negotiate.

Think in terms of the cell phone minutes on your monthly plan. Wouldn't it have been nice to check in and assess the history of your cell phone usage and adjust your plan three to six months after you got your first cell phone? The cell phone company is certainly not going to suggest this if they're making overage charges or if the original plan covers more minutes than you have been using. You need to take this into your own hands.

Long-term contracts are often a key part of large outsourcing deals. These may be 5 to 10 years or more, and it is important to look at the contract with that in mind. For instance, look at the technological innovations in HR in the last five years. How is this

---

* Sunk Cost: a cost that has been incurred and cannot be recovered.

** Fixed Cost: a cost that does not vary with volume level or activity or output.

factored into the contract? Will the vendors need to recoup their investments and, subsequently, cause your organization to be several years behind in HR technology?

What about shifts in organizational size? Will the contract scale up or down and does it allow for shifts in the size of your organization's population? If you go through a downsizing and ten percent of the workforce is cut, how will this be reflected in the contract?

Even if your employee population remains the same, the number of transactions may dramatically increase or decrease. For example, over the last several years, web-based employee self-service has sharply diminished the telephone call volume of transactional HR services. This would, expectedly, lead to a reduction in the number of people required for call centers. How would this shift be reflected in your contract?

Of course, not all questions can be answered as you set out to define the relationship within clear contractual obligations; therefore, the ability to update and refine the relationship as time goes on is critical. Provision for this must be built into the contract without diminishing the commitment of your organization in the partnership, and by taking into consideration the risks on the part of the vendor. That is the balance that must be reached.

Financial Evaluation of RFPs

When trying to compare dollars to dollars in outsourcing agreements, many organizations simply stack up outsourcing contracts against each other on a straight dollar comparison. If service levels are not to be taken into account this might work, but this is rarely the case.

There are also more sophisticated methods to look at the financial aspects of an outsourcing arrangement and these factors need to be carefully considered with your CFO or controller. Some of these include:

- Return on Equity
- Return on Assets
- Cash-flow implications.

Activity-Based Costing

Activity-Based Costing is a type of accounting that lends itself well to accurately gauging the true costs of specific processes. This can be especially valuable as you consider outsourcing all or only parts of a process.

Activity-Based Costing (ABC) looks at the individual steps in a process and not just at the overhead costs of a department or process. Traditional Cost Accounting simply takes overhead cost and divides it by transactions (e.g., total Recruiting Department costs of $1,000,000 divided by 400 hires = $2,500 Cost-Per-Hire).

Activity-Based Costing breaks the process down by identifying activities that take place and then looking at how these activities consume resources.

This example shows how different types of jobs consume different levels of resources based on their varying volume and the amount of effort the activities take.

Recruiting							
Activity	Total Cost $	Sales-people	Cost $	Administrative Staff	Cost $	Managers/ Directors	Cost $
Sourcing Candidates	40000	25	20000	20	10000	6	10000
Screening Candidates	15000	25	7500	20	2500	6	5000
Selection	15000	10	15000	10	2500	3	7500
Hiring	5000	3	2000	5	1000	2	2000
Onboarding	10000	5	5000	3	3000	2	2000
	95000		49500		19000		26500

FIGURE 11-1

ABC can yield excellent insight into the true cost structure of a process, but figuring this out can take a lot of time and energy. ABC normally makes sense only in a large organization, where the effort and cost can be justified. You might discuss this with your CFO or finance and accounting team to determine if it would be a financially logical endeavor.

HR Outsourcing Key #3:

Allocate Sufficient Resources to Manage the Outsourcing Relationship Effectively

An overlooked aspect of outsourcing is the internal resources required by the organization to manage the outsourcing partnership. The additional work is normally tacked on to the responsibilities of an existing staff person. This approach does not dignify the critical nature of this role. Nor does it address the "growing pains" aspect of an outsourcing partnership that will happen most certainly in the beginning as change management and adoption issues surface. There will also be additional work required to develop an effective working relationship between the customer organization and the provider, which may take months or longer.

Managing the Outsourcing Relationship

The level of involvement in day-to-day issues must be carefully managed by the internal contact person in the organization. The key here is to manage the relationship while not getting drawn into performing the role that should rest within the domain of the outsourcing provider. It undermines the business case for outsourcing if the internal person ends up doing more work than was originally planned, and also ends up doing work that should be handled by the outsourcing provider. This can be especially pervasive when the former front-line HR employee is tasked with managing the relationship with the vendor who is performing his previous job duties. The employee easily gravitates toward doing aspects of what were his old job, because it is comfortable. But the employee should only focus on managing the vendor relationship, not managing the vendor's daily functions for the organization.

If the new outsourcing paradigm is to work financially then these potential additional internal labor costs must be carefully contained and managed.

Is Outsourcing a Solution to Your Workload?

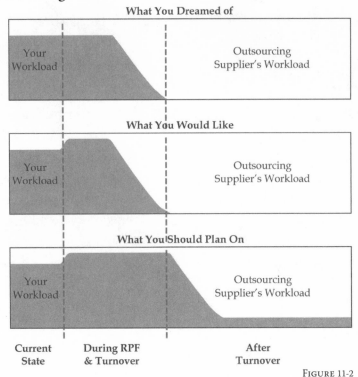

FIGURE 11-2

HR Outsourcing Key #4:

Perform Due Diligence in Selecting an Outsourcing Supplier and Constructing a Partnership

Conducting due diligence involves more than selecting the proper vendor to partner with. It includes checking references, financial stability, and the ability to meet your current and future needs. It also means meticulously clarifying the relationship, including milestones, measures of success, transitioning communications strategies, and a clearly defined exit strategy should the partnership not work out.

The vendor selection process normally starts with a Request for Proposal (RFP) or a Request for Information (RFI), which is an even more preliminary step, to gather information to construct an RFP and to identify logical choices of vendors to include in the RFP process.

A comprehensive RFP includes the following elements:

- Statement or purpose
- Background information
- Scope of work
- Terms of contract
- Deliverables
- Performance standards
- Payments, incentives, and penalties
- General contractual conditions
- Special contractual conditions
- Requirements-for-proposal preparation
- Organization contacts and hours scheduled
- Evaluation and award process.

References and Background Checking

Just as you scrutinize job candidates, you need to do a similar amount of detective work about potential outsourcing partners.

Ask for customer references, both from current customers and from customers who have terminated their service. Get straight answers about why former customers parted ways with them and validate this by speaking with those customers.

Do an Internet search on the outsourcing company, using various search engines, to get a sense of anything that might be a red flag, such as past or pending litigation. If the company is relatively young and there are a couple of key founders, check their names as well. What you might find are red flags from a similar, previously run company, and this organization may simply be an attempt to start fresh.

Depending on the size of the organization, if there are a few key founders, get a sense of their backgrounds. Are they industry veterans? Or are they just jumping on the HR outsourcing trend?

Your controller or CFO should be involved as you look at the financial stability of the outsourcing company. Check banking and credit references, and look very carefully at whether the organization is a startup or if it is venture funded. This harkens back to the dot-com days, but don't be afraid ask the questions:

- Are you profitable?
- Since what date?
- If not, when do you expect to be profitable?
- On what do you base this expectation?

The Cultural Aspect of a Vendor Partnership

The question must be asked, "Does this vendor function in a way that is conducive to our culture?" The answer to this question can lead in several different directions. If the vendor has a more refined and structured culture, this could help raise the bar for the organization to gravitate to that level. It can also put off organizational team members who are used to a more casual structure. The answer to this question posed above must come from the leadership of the organization. Is a cultural shift desired? If so, what is the desired direction? And, is the vendor's culture compatible with that desired direction?

Cultural understanding is also something to carefully consider in the use of offshore vendors or facilities. Depending on the level of interaction needed with local employees, an offshore person may be ill-suited to effectively interact on a social level with people even if his or her tactical ability is adequate. This might be broadly cast into the category of communications skills, but it goes deeper than language ability and strikes at the nature of how interactions take place (e.g., confrontation, negotiation, sensitivity to the power structure in the organization).

Data Security, Privacy, and Outsourcing

Data security should be an issue to carefully explore, since liability for identity theft and privacy issues are of great concern to organizations. This is a simple matter of business sense for vendors and it is a key liability issue that many in-house organizations may not think about as deeply as they should. An internal HR person may not get hit as heavily about data security from line-managers or senior management, but a sales rep for an outsourcing firm will and needs to have solid answers. It is incumbent upon you (the customer) to ask and verify. This is definitely an area where you need to pull your IT staff in on the process for their insight and guidance. You need to carefully scrutinize this area and pull in appropriate individuals and departments that have the knowledge and capability to verify your vendor's data security protocols.

It is also important to consider the possible legal implications when data goes offshore to outsourced vendors or to their subcontractors. Privacy laws and other laws may not apply where you have data being transmitted to other countries, and, if there are protections, they may be difficult to enforce.

There will be data that your organization may want to keep in-house and private, such as negative performance reviews and other sensitive personal data. The questions arise as to what risk this would pose and what additional work it would create. These issues should be carefully considered before you craft an outsourcing strategy.

Play the "What If" Game

While a strong contract and service level agreement are helpful in covering your due diligence, it is difficult to foresee every possible scenario. Some additional probing questions are in order. I call this the "What if" game. Explore what will happen when certain likely or even unlikely events might transpire. For example:

- Turnover within the outsourcing company team, such as an account manager, project manager, or other key staff
- Natural disaster
- Potential lawsuits and what responsibilities and roles might be taken.

Some of these items will be covered in the outsourcing contract and service level agreement, but the "What if" game can help you further understand the experience and comfort level that an outsourcing provider might have in dealing with certain situations. Think of it as Behavioral Interviewing 101: *Past performance predicts future performance.* The outsourcing provider should be able to cite specific examples of how it has handled unforeseen challenges in the past with other organizations. This can give you at least some idea of how the provider will deal with unforeseen challenges in the future. This gives you a chance to pierce their "marketing" bubble and review the depth of their resources and capabilities.

HR Outsourcing Key #5:

Be Prepared for the Outsourcing Arrangement to End

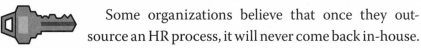 Some organizations believe that once they outsource an HR process, it will never come back in-house. This is far from the truth. In fact, almost one in four companies have brought outsourced HR functions back in-house—with over a third citing unachieved cost savings, and the other almost-two-thirds citing poor service levels.* Here I come back to your process maps as tools to preserve organizational knowledge about how you've done things in the past. If the payroll manager is long gone, for example, do you have anything that preserves organizational knowledge about your particular needs and requirements? This could be used to create another RFP, or to look at bringing the service back in-house based on new factors.

What Happens When the Honeymoon Is Over?

After a reasonable amount of time into an outsourcing contract, the anticipated gains just may not be achieved. The reduction in

---

* "HR Outsourcing Continues to Boom as Organizations Gain Experience and Reap Benefits." *Business Wire,* April 18, 2005.

costs and workload may not be present or have simply been replaced by other costs and other work, resulting in too little net gain. At this point, hard questions must be asked:

- What is wrong?
- Are there indications that this can and will improve?
- How much of the blame can be attributed to your own actions or inactions? For what must the vendor be held responsible?
- Based on the historical experience, should you continue to have trust and confidence in this vendor?
- What are your risks by continuing the contract? By ending the contract?
- How do the contract terms address ending the relationship?
- What are your options?
- Should you consider bringing this process back in-house? Why?
- What benefits can be realized in shifting to another vendor? What are the risks?

Scope Creep in the Outsourcing Relationship

As you look back at how important clear requirements and responsibilities are in the beginning stages of forging a deal toward a relationship, it is beneficial for both parties to understand how the scope of the relationship might have evolved over time. Responsibility for this must be mutually undertaken, and hiding behind the contract in these cases may be a situation where one wins the battle but loses the war.

The outsourcing firm may be spending resources to address obscure business objectives that were not evident in the beginning and not part of the original scope of work. While the outsourcing provider does not want to take a *not-my-job* approach, serving these needs may be at the cost to their profit margin. It is incumbent upon both parties to acknowledge this and to identify some equitable resolution that meets both the customer's business needs and compensates the outsourcing provider accordingly.

When Things Go Bad

A clear and unambiguous contract can be invaluable in making an outsourcing arrangement work. Sometimes things don't work, though, and that contingency must be acknowledged and included in the contract. Have your legal team review carefully what happens if the outsourcing relationship doesn't go as planned and ends prematurely.

There are two areas in the contract that need special attention and these are: *relationship continuation and transition clauses.*

Relationship Continuation aka Business Continuation Clauses

These clauses address what happens when a contract ends, and allows a *business-as-usual* situation to continue until matters are resolved. This can be very useful in contract negotiation renewals or when the relationship with a vendor is ended at the end of a contract term. It provides a time buffer to make a smoother transition to another vendor or, perhaps, to bring the outsourced services back in-house again.

The more dependent an organization is on a vendor, the more critical this clause is. This business continuation should also not be contingent upon mutual agreement by both parties. The customer needs to have the ability to continue the contract for a reasonable amount of time (whether this is 90 days, six months, or one year will depend upon the level of dependence and complexity of the relationship).

Transition Clauses

The transition clause can be closely tied to the business continuation clause, but it should be looked at as a separate issue. While the business continuation clause deals with time, the transition clause addresses more of the *how.* This clause makes sure that the relationship remains amicable and functional during a period of transition of the contract. For example, in switching to a new HRIS vendor, the transition clause should stipulate an orderly exchange of customer data to be efficiently migrated to the new system. This clause should attempt to sustain the same vendor relationship on the way *out of* the business relationship as with *entering into* it.

Professional Employer Organizations—HR Business Process Outsourcing for Small Organizations

A strong outsourcing option for small organizations is the *Professional Employer Organization* (PEO).

A PEO acts as the employer of record and allows companies to forgo having a full-time human resources staff, or forcing senior management or other staff to undertake human resources management activities that they may not be trained to do. This can be especially attractive for very small organizations (under 20 employees) and for those that are larger but which may have difficulty in providing basic HR services. The PEO utilizes the aggregate population of many smaller organizations to achieve economies of scale in providing market competitive benefits. In many cases, but not all, organizations with greater than a hundred employees will often see a diminished business case for a PEO compared to a full-time human resources person.

The PEO often handles payroll and payroll taxes, benefits, and all workers' compensation issues. Additional human resources activities are often available and can be purchased on an as-needed or monthly retainer basis. Again, especially in small businesses, allowing the organization to focus on its core activity can be even more critical, and outsourcing the human resources function can make the most sense.

Shared Services: An Alternative to Outsourcing

A centralized approach to providing HR services has been a growing trend in many large organizations that have economies of scale. By providing a centralized *Shared Service*, organizations see this as a more desirable option than outsourcing.

In this model, the different divisions or parts of a large organization, which might have had their own independent HR structure, utilize a central shared HR service. The HR entity is set up almost like an outsourcing provider and may allocate its costs back to the different business units based on their utilization of the service. Through this, economies of scale, as well as uniformity across the organization, drive cost savings by having no duplicated technology or integration problems between business units.

Final Thoughts

Whether your approach to outsourcing has been incremental or your organization is looking at full BPO (shifting the end-to-end human resources function outside) the approach to outsourcing must be careful and strategic.

While many organizations explore outsourcing, some find, after careful examination, that refining their existing operations is the best solution—or outsourcing is merely integrated into this improved HR model. In addition, many organizations have been forced to switch vendors or even bring outsourced operations back in-house because the promise of outsourcing remained unfilled.

You need to be prepared for all of these possibilities.

THE FUTURE OF OUTSOURCING

HR Professionals Must Take a Proactive Role

The culture of outsourcing is one that HR practitioners need to embrace. HR professionals must become change agents, and take a proactive role in exploring outsourcing options. With this will come inevitable changes for the HR profession and the shift for some HR professionals to working for an outsourcing company. Those HR professionals who remain internally at an organization will most likely function at an elevated level, fulfilling a much more strategic role.

It is important to be knowledgeable about the risks and opportunities of outsourcing, and to be approachable about the topic, whether you are personally for or against outsourcing. Otherwise, you may find yourself not sitting at the decision-making table, with the CEO and CFO making decisions about the HR department's future without your input. I see this as one of the most dangerous potential scenarios for HR but, in part, HR does have some control over this.

HR professionals need to make themselves knowledgeable about outsourcing vendor options. What services are available to the organization? Who are the key vendors to provide them?

HR's role may shift to that of a gatekeeper, as the liaison between the organization and the outsourcing partner. To act as point person between internal customers, senior management, and the vendor, the internal HR person must have enough process knowledge to correctly measure success and anticipate future risks and opportunities. (In the following section, I will discuss some of the challenges that this presents for the HR profession as a whole.)

Outsourcing is definitely here to stay. It continues to gather momentum because it improves the strategic processes of organizations. This shift in how organizations handle their human resources activities will dictate a new skill set that emerging human resources professionals will need to have if they're functioning within the organization and not working for an outsourcer.

This shift will entail moving from the daily service of customers and performing the transactional aspects of the HR, to the management of the relationship with vendors and monitoring the service levels of internal customers. In addition, there will continue to be the need to make sure current and future activities are aligned with HR and organizational strategy.

 KEY THOUGHT

> Any attitudinal resistance to HR outsourcing may result in the pursuit of outsourcing taking place without HR being present.

Impact of Outsourcing and the HR Profession

Historically, there is a revolving door that occurs in the outsourcing world. We can look to the example of recruiters, where it is commonly held that contract or third-party recruiters tend to earn more than their corporate counterparts. While this is partially due to the premium paid for temporary work for contract recruiters and to the more incentive-based compensation structure, the differences in pay can be dramatic. What we see, though, is not necessarily a one-way exodus of corporate recruiters learning the ropes and then defecting to higher-paying third-party recruiting roles. There are many who start as third-party recruiters and migrate to become staff recruiters inside companies. This may involve a trade-off of lower-upside potential but more stable income—and, depending on who you talk to, it may or may not include less stress.

The world of outsourcing is not a one-way door either, with HR professionals being recruited to work for the outsourcing companies and outsourcing employees being recruited by their customers to work in-house.

These shifts will be driven by the demand for HR professionals inside companies to manage the outsourcing relationship, and by the demand for experienced HR professionals to work for the out-sourcing firms:

- Companies will desire HR professionals who understand the inside workings of the outsourcing firms and can manage the contract better vis-a-vis their understanding of areas to push and what they might be able to negotiate in terms of service and cost management.

- Outsourcing firms will desire HR professionals who under-stand the inner workings and culture of corporate clients.

- And, HR professionals may be drawn to the opportunity to get to be "The Customer" by working on the company side— or, to the diversity in assignments they may experience by working for an outsourcing vendor.

Something else to consider is the supply-and-demand paradigm that will likely take place, which may result in a shrinking supply of internal HR people coming up the ranks into management roles. Last summer's HR intern who just graduated may be well suited to be a benefits coordinator, but certainly lacks the experience and capability to meet the challenges of managing your outsourced-ben-efits administration partner, and to act as the internal point person on benefits. So the question arises: "Where will this skills gap be filled and how will entry-level HR people gain the critical experience necessary to fulfill this management role inside the company?" It will most likely mean that many will commence their careers work-ing for an outsourcing provider.

As you consider the off-shoring aspect in HR outsourcing, many of these lower-level positions may be going offshore, compounding the supply issue for experienced HR managers in the domestic market.

Increasingly, as some HR professionals wonder about their jobs and worry about the impact of outsourcing on their careers, I think back to a saying I once heard: "Don't concentrate on being employed or not—concentrate on being employable."

As you think about your future career in HR, it is something to keep in mind. Are you and your skill sets what the future HR market needs? You might be wise to keep an eye on the hiring trends of outsourcing providers (jobs hired for, required skills, etc.) whether you are on the corporate side, or vice-versa.

CHANGE MANAGEMENT AND PROCESS IMPROVEMENT

Change is inevitable—except from a vending machine.

(Robert C. Gallagher, Chairman of the Board/Director, Associated Banc-Corp)

WHEN initiating any kind of process improvement, it is critical to give proper attention to the change-*management* aspects of creating change. In short, you need to figure out how to get from the current state to the desired "improved" state in your processes.

To accomplish this, you need to spend some time identifying and addressing the following:

- Where the change will need to take place
- What that change will entail
- How to get from your current state to your desired state.

Later in this chapter, I will look at tool called a Force Field Analysis. After that, I will address in greater detail the human element in change, and I will offer some suggestions on how to work within the overall psychology of the resistance to change.

Where Change Can Take Place

Change may take place at many different levels, including:

- Organizational levels
- Process levels
- Job or employee performance levels.

Figure 12-1 shows these different levels and identifies some specific areas at each, where change might need to occur.

- Input/Supplier Requirements
- Information Flow
- Work Process
- Measures
- Performance and Management Systems

Organizational
Process
Job/Employee Level

- Strategy
- Policy
- Values and Behaviors
- Organizational Structure
- Goals and Rewards

- Roles and Responsibilities
- Required Skills
- Training
- Job and Human Performance System

FIGURE 12-1

What Change Will Entail

In chapter 5, we discussed processes and how to identify a current state and a desired (future) state as you work to improve the processes. As you now consider the changes that take place at an organizational and job performer level, a more generic view can be surmised of the current and desired states. The change that must take place between these is the *solution path*.

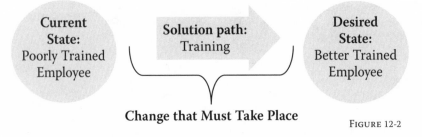

Current State: Poorly Trained Employee

Solution path: Training

Desired State: Better Trained Employee

Change that Must Take Place

FIGURE 12-2

How to Get From the Current State to the Desired State

Moving from where you are to where you want to be is an activity normally easier said than done. To accomplish this move, I will look at two key areas:

- Understanding and addressing the factors influencing change
- Dealing specifically with the human element of change.

Invisible Force Fields: Understanding and Overcoming Why New Programs Receive Resistance

Invisible force fields have been a staple of science fiction and superhero comics for many years. These insidious phenomena appear out of nowhere and somehow thwart our heroes from accomplishing what they need to do, each adding a new element of challenge and drama.

A similar phenomenon appears in many process-improvement or re-engineering efforts. We ingeniously simplify and improve a process or adeptly replace a manual endeavor with technology that improves the process. Yet, despite these best efforts, we are thwarted by slow-adapting departments, line-managers resistant to change, by individuals who are technologically challenged, or by those who refuse to explore new technologies. Just as we have managed to plug the original proverbial leak, others spring open.

The root of this is often a *generalized resistance to change*—a simple fact of human nature. However, there are many other factors that can contribute to this resistance as well. These must be considered and weighed against the benefits. All of these factors must be considered not only from the organization's view, but also from the standpoint of the people adopting change, or affected by it. It is individuals or departments that throw up these force fields, and the root reasons must be uncovered and addressed.

Force Field Analysis

Force Field Analysis is a useful technique for looking at the different forces that exist for and against a change. It is a graphic and analytical method of weighing pros and cons.

Doing a Force Field Analysis is another one of those tools that may seem remedial at first, but the change-management aspect of most process-improvement efforts is where many projects go astray, leaving the project team frustrated and eroding the improvements that were sought.

Since you will be addressing a cycle of projects in HR, the Force Field Analysis can help you choose and prioritize projects. By carrying out the Analysis, you can plan to strengthen the forces supporting a decision, and reduce the impact of opposition to it. Thus, Force Field Analysis can help you to work out how to improve its probability of success.

There are basically two forces at work:

Driving: Forces that push toward a solution

Restraining: Forces that inhibit improvements, or try to reinforce the status quo.

These forces could also be called *For vs. Against, or Pro vs. Con.*

When the strength of the driving forces is about equal to the restraining forces, then a *status quo,* or balance, is created. To move the status quo forward, the relative strength of the forces must be changed.

To accomplish this, you have two choices:

- To reduce the strength of the forces opposing a project, or
- To increase the forces pushing a project.

In many cases, the best solution is a combination of the two: improving driving forces and reducing restraining forces.

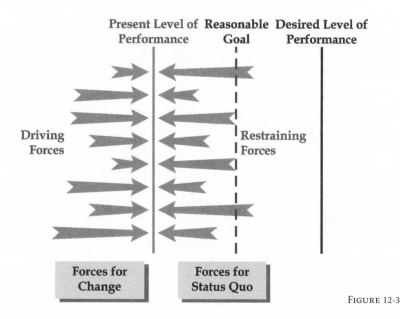

FIGURE 12-3

QUICK TIP

Doing a Force Field Analysis

The **Force Field Analysis** is a helpful technique for examining all the forces for and against a plan. It helps you to weigh the importance of these factors and decide whether a plan is worth implementing.

To carry out a Force Field Analysis, take the following five steps discussed below. Begin by listing all forces for change in one column, and all forces against change in another column.

1. Assign a score to each force between 1 and 5, where 1 is low or weak and 5 is high or strong.

2. Total the scores in each column.

3. Draw a diagram showing the forces for and against change, and show the strength of each force as a number next to it.

4. Examine each force and determine ways that the score can be changed. (How can restraining forces be reduced? How can driving forces be increased?)

In the following diagram, the forces *For Change* are shown on the left and given a weighted score, while the forces *Against Change* are shown on the right with a corresponding weighted score. The total for change equals 11 and the total against change equals 10. While the forces for change outweigh those against change, this is still too close to catalyze a change initiative. This means that each factor needs to be looked at again, and the team needs to determine ways to increase the forces for and reduce the factors against.

Force Field Analysis Example

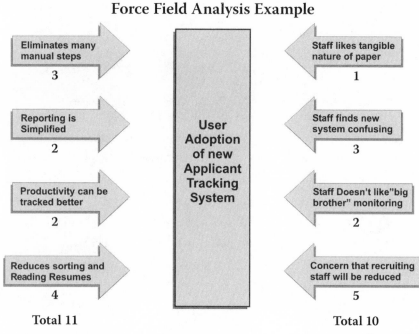

FIGURE 12-4

As you look at the scores in Figure 12-4, there are slightly more forces driving change than there are restraining change. The score of 11 to 10 is very close, though, and the ratio needs to be shifted to increase the move toward change.

The reporting in the new Applicant Tracking System shown above brings up both a driving force (simplified reporting) and a restraining force (staff doesn't like "big brother" monitoring). By working on this issue and training the staff on how reporting will save them time in not having to try to justify all the work that they do, staff may become more accepting of the new reporting functionality, see how it can help them in their jobs, and become less suspicious that the reporting will be used against them.

The result:

Driving Force: Reporting is Simplified	**Result:** Increase driving force by 1 to 3
Restraining Force: Staff doesn't like "big brother" monitoring	**Result:** Reduce restraining force by 1 to 1
	Net Result: Shift from 11:10 to 12:9

The Psychology of Change: Some Suggestions

Once the factors promoting and resisting change have been identified, you can start trying to counter the resistance issues, and work on selling or increasing the perceived benefits of adopting the change.

Unfortunately, the human element brings a vital and tricky variable into the mix when implementing change.

Ignoring this variable commonly results in an organization simply announcing change. A training schedule is posted, as well as whatever else seems like the simplest path to get from problem state to solution state. If there is resistance, company memos are distributed, or even terse emails, demanding that new procedures be adopted. While this is a common avenue to getting things done, the need for it underscores the red flags that an organization may have ignored in developing the new procedure or implementing technology. Though it is commonly accepted that people are often inherently resistant to change, there is always a need to understand any deeper meanings driving resistance.

The following are some general suggestions.

Spend Extra Time Understanding the Implications of Change

One of the simplest ways to identify and address change resistance is to ask those involved if they perceive that the new process will benefit, or somehow negatively affect, them. This check-in may be done in one-on-one interviews, focus groups, or surveys. Some sample questions are:

> "Will this change make your job easier or more difficult in any way?"

> "Do you think this is really beneficial to the company? To you?"

> "Do you think this will hurt your paycheck? Productivity? Sanity?"

"Do you think this is a good plan?"

"Do you think other people will have any problems with this?"

"What do you think is going to be your biggest challenge if we do this?"

The answers to these questions may be surprising, but they'll certainly enlighten you!

Consider How You Are Driving Behavior

As you think about changing behavior, you may be able to apply an additional model to the Force Field Analysis, which includes elements that reinforce behavior (reinforcers) and elements that punish behavior (punishers).

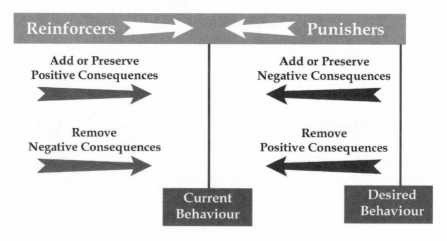

FIGURE 12-5

Remember: A new program can have wonderful benefits to an organization—but you need to realize that a new program should foster a symbiotic relationship between the organization and its employees. It is crucial that employees' interests are properly aligned, and conjoined, with those of the organization.

Sometimes change has a negative effect on individuals. This needs to be carefully considered and adjusted. A loyal employee may be all for a change that saves the company money—right up to the point where the employee sees that the savings is being generated by taking it out of his or her own pocket. It is fine when the cut comes from the pockets of vendors, or by reducing waste, but when the employee has become accustomed to a certain paycheck and this change suddenly slashes overtime or incentive pay, expect your new program to hit a force field.

Profit sharing can be a means to help overcome this, but expect an employee to weigh personal returns against those of the company. In other words, the prospect of another $500 profit sharing bonus at the end of the year is nice, but an employee will quickly do the math after seeing a loss of $200 every paycheck that was once paid out in overtime.

The result can be slowdowns and other actions that undermine the improvements the new process would have otherwise created.

To best manage and ensure the smooth and successful adoption of change, the rewards (reinforcers) to the adopters must be clearly communicated and perhaps increased, while the negative effects (punishments) must be limited, reduced, or otherwise mitigated. The economics of this could feasibly be split, such as offering a pay increase to offset the lost overtime, which can serve to compensate the employee for having to work fewer hours than in the past. There is no set formula for this, but it is something that must be considered when implementing change that employees may view as punishment.

Show Empathy When There Is an Impasse

There will come times, unavoidably, when the good of the organization must be put ahead of the negative impact on individuals. Sometimes just acknowledging the negative effects up front can make an organization seem more sensitive to issues and can diminish some of the employees' frustrations and resistance. Though they may also have their own interests in mind, employees are often understanding of business necessities, if they are informed of them. The key is to clearly define the problem, establish what the options were, and explain why this was the chosen solution. If you can demonstrate a genuine effort on the part of the organization to having tried to avoid or work around what the employee perceives as the negative aspects of the solution, the employee is more likely to accept it. This is also a key time to listen to feedback. Another solution or compromise may be suggested by the employee at this point that was not previously considered.

 KEY THOUGHTS

- As you think about improving your HR operations, be mindful of understanding the changes that will take place. Then, carefully construct a plan for how to manage these changes.

- To effectively manage change and to create a plan, you need to understand where the change will take place, what it will entail, and what factors influence its adoption or resistance.

- A Force Field Analysis can be very helpful in understanding the forces working for and against change.

- You also need to be mindful of the human elements of change.

- Consider the impacts to the individual, and how you are driving the behaviors that you wish to change.

CONTROL

The control phase is one of the most overlooked and often glossed over aspects of process improvement efforts—yet, it is among the most crucial.

At this point, you have identified and have implemented improvements in your operations. This may be through process improvement, implementing HR technology, or through outsourcing.

Now you need to make these improvements stick.

The real benefits from your improvements will come as they accrue over time, and you must put controls in place to maintain your success.

SERVICE LEVEL MANAGEMENT

INTERNAL SERVICE LEVEL AGREEMENTS IN HR

RETURN ON INVESTMENT AND HR

MAINTAINING EXCELLENCE

Define 〉 Measure 〉 Analyze 〉 Improve 〉 Control

13

SERVICE LEVEL
MANAGEMENT

A verbal contract isn't worth the paper it's written on.

(Samuel Goldwyn, motion picture producer, 1882–1974)

A s discussed earlier, as outsourcing continues, HR professionals need to become more familiar with structuring and
managing service level agreements with vendors—the written frameworks that define what acceptable service performance
will look like. In addition, the adoption of service level agreements
for use internally (between HR and its customers) is becoming
more prevalent. Both of these issues fall under a broader umbrella
of *Service Level Management.*

In this chapter I will discuss service level management and service level agreements (SLA). Then, in the next chapter, I will discuss
SLAs in more depth, and offer suggestions as to how they can be
applied to internal service agreements between HR and its customers.

What Is Service Level Management?

Service Level Management is the effort to manage the quality
and quantity of services delivered. There are four objectives of SLM:

- Establishing commitments

- Monitoring the performance against commitments

- Responding quickly when commitments have been missed
  or are in danger of being missed

• Regularly reporting on the actual service levels in terms of performance vs. commitments.

Service Level Management (SLM) and Service Level Agreements (SLA) are not the same things. Service level management is the concept, and a service level agreement is the *articulation of the agreement between the service provider and the customer.* Service level management focuses on a holistic process for better serving the customer, including managing needs, resources, metrics, priorities, and consistency.

In short: *You can practice Service Level Management without a Service Level Agreement, but having an SLA without instituting SLM is a recipe for disaster.*

What Is a Service Level Agreement?

The Service Level Agreement is an agreement between the supplier of a service and the user of that service. The SLA defines:

• Availability of the service to the user

• Performance targets of various components of the user's workload

• Boundaries of guaranteed performance and availability

• Measurement and reporting mechanisms

• Cost of the service (where cost is an agreed to component of the SLA).

Service level agreements in and of themselves will not improve service levels or change behaviors around service. They are merely a guide to get all parties on the same page to understand and agree upon what good performance should look like.

SLAs can range dramatically from very broadly worded and basic measures of performance to the incredibly precise—and may also vary from user to user, even within the same organization.

SLAs—Good for both Vendors and Customers

Without taking the time to clarify the relationship through a service level agreement and spelling out each party's roles and responsibilities, both vendor and customer put themselves at risk. If there is no SLA, the relationship is held together on two assumptions:

- Customers relying on the vendor's desire to keep their business
- Vendors relying on their customers to have reasonable expectations.

Having a written service level agreement is a critical tool in the service provider/customer relationship.

Since HR encompasses a multitude of services (benefits administration, training, recruiting, etc.), broad-based service level agreements are inherently difficult to apply. While well-intentioned, these vague service targets are destined to fail because they try to apply a generic solution to a multitude of situations.

Each particular process within HR must be looked at independently, and each one needs to be examined to determine *if* and *how* an SLA can be applied to it. There are many factors that will influence the SLA. These include:

- Different users with different requirements for the same service
- Different users with different demand or usage of the same service
- Different values associated with characteristics of the service such as speed, quality, availability, and other factors
- Different costs may be associated with the service that HR will provide to the different users of its services (department charge-backs, etc.).

Structure of a Service Level Agreement

A Service Level Agreement has some key areas, including:

Objective   The reason for the service agreement.

Definition A clear and concise definition of the service and desired level.

Method   A description of how performance will be measured.

Timing   When performance will be reviewed.

Action   What happens when service levels are not met.

KEYS TO SERVICE LEVEL AGREEMENTS

The following are some key elements to think about when crafting and negotiating an SLA.

Defining Is the Key to a Service Level Agreement

There is a certain amount of adversity to be expected when negotiating the specific measurements of an SLA. Vendors often want the SLA as loose as possible, allowing them to function in a more flexible environment. That is not to say that most vendors want to shirk their responsibilities, but that they would rather not be harnessed with too many requirements and constraints in how they do their job. The customers would like maximum protection to guarantee performance levels and results. Depending on the situation, the customer may or may not care about *how* things get done—just *that* they get done.

To be effective, a service level agreement must clarify the subject so that both service provider and customer are drawing on a common base of understanding, with the mutual objective of satisfying the customer's needs. An SLA should define and address the following areas:

- Type of service
- Definition of service
- Volume
- Timeliness
- Availability
- Reliability
- Compensation for Service (if any)
- Measurement
- Date for review or renegotiation.

Think about Future Fluctuations in Volume

Volume is a critical aspect to consider in service level quality. Without understanding and agreeing to the volume that is to be expected, how can service levels be guaranteed by the provider? HR normally has a budget for fixed labor costs. Events outside of HR, such as unexpectedly high turnover in another department, may require additional, unplanned work on the part of HR that needs to be considered like any other changing business condition. The same economic model will apply to an outsourcing partner and may have a corresponding impact on service levels.

In thinking about volume, the time distribution is important to understand and agree to as well. Sixty hires that are evenly distributed over a year equal only five per month, but if that 60 is required in one quarter or one month, this must be taken into account when gauging service levels. This is why the SLA is a living document. It needs to be constantly revisited and adjusted based on the ever-changing business conditions.

There is sometimes a disconnection between HR and the users of HR's services, which can also translate to a disconnect with outsourcing providers. The first is often a gap in expectations between the HR staff and business users. The second is that many HR metrics are gauged to the entire business and performance of the HR departments, and are not measurements that are germane to the individual business users. The number of people trained or the average cost-per-hire means something to the business as a whole but not necessarily to the individual business user of HR's services. As a result, HR may be hitting organizational metrics, yet failing to meet the business needs and priorities of its customers.

However, establishing a multitude of internal service level metrics may not be worthwhile. This approach could have a *paralysis by analysis* effect, and eat up precious resources in measuring, tracking, and reporting on what may not be useful metrics. The goal here is to *find a balance between effort expended and information gathered* so as to create a positive return on investment of the time spent.

Since many of HR's services still happen offline, they are not as easy to track as services that take place in the IT department, for example—where trouble tickets and server up-times are easier to report on and measure without an unreasonable amount of labor involved.

Time Is a Critical Element to Consider

 Before you sign off on an SLA, you should consider the following time issues:

- Hours of service
- Response time
- Resolution time of issues.

Hours of Service

It is a basic issue, but the hours of service need to be clarified, including such components as: Are there specific hours between which service will be provided (say, 8 a.m.–5 p.m.)? What if services are needed after close of business? What about multiple time zones being serviced?

Response Time

How are your response times calculated? Is it from time of request to acknowledgment of the issue? Or, resolution of the issue? For instance, are you called back within four hours with the acknowl-edgment that your issue is being looked at? Or, is the issue *fixed* within four hours?

What if response time extends past the close of business? For instance, what if you have a 4-hour response guarantee and call about an issue at 4:00 p.m. with service until 5:00 p.m.? Does that mean that the three remaining hours begin counting at 8:00 a.m. the next morning, meaning resolution by 11:00 a.m.? If there are multiple locations and parties involved on both the client and the vendor sides and the locations span different time zones, by which clock will time be calculated?

Resolution Time

Customers want their issues resolved. Well-meaning attention to problems that do not lead to resolution still fall short in the custom-er's eyes. So it is important to track both response and resolution.

This opens up a difficult area to qualify in advance—how long will it take to resolve the problem? Rather than slotting in arbitrary or cushioned response times as a blanket for all possible issues, the various types of issues can be classified and assigned times accord-ingly. A better method still is to measure against agreed-upon or negotiated times. That is to say, the time for resolution is determined on a case-by-case basis, negotiated with the customer, agreed to by both parties, and then measured for accuracy.

Carrots and Sticks: Make Sure Incentives Are Built into SLAs in Addition to Penalties

A critical element of any Service Level Agreement is some sort of penalty that is imposed when agreed-upon service targets are not met. This can be fairly straightforward when there is an outside vendor that is billing for services—for example, a two or five or 10% reduction in last month's bill if service levels are not achieved. In the next chapter, I will discuss some of the main issues that arise when utilizing SLAs internally.

While many SLAs have potential penalties built into them to guard against poor performance, incentives should also be built in as a management tool. Basic behavioral psychology teaches that rewards always work better than punishment. Keep this in mind as you construct or review your SLAs. Remember: *You are trying to drive favorable behavior.* Incentives can take the form of sharing a percentage of operational savings, or some other financial benefit.

Incentives for Service Above and Beyond Target Levels

Exceeding service expectations will normally come at the cost of some resources—whether they are in labor or other expenses. In a profit-driven environment like that of the outsourcer, if needed service levels have already been met, what is the incentive to the vendor to spend additional resources to increase service levels further?

If the customer receives some appreciable benefit from this increased service level, additional incentives to the supplier may be in order. The test here is *whether or not a business benefit is created that translates into some financial benefit for the organization.* If there is no ultimate financial benefit to the customer, no financial incentives should be passed on to the supplier.

For example, a supplier in the staffing process that helps expedite the process above and beyond expected service levels for hiring a salesperson on quota may be a candidate for an incentive, since this can be translated into greater than expected revenue gains by getting that salesperson onboard and producing revenue sooner than expected. On the other hand, an HR technology vendor that increases up-time of a hosted software application from a 99.9 to 99.99 percent may not be a good candidate for the incentive as this may not easily translate into a business benefit that can be quantified with a dollar amount.

By sharing the wealth with suppliers (when applicable), the customer reinforces the behavior that is beneficial to the customer's organization and subsequently encourages the supplier to invest in the relationship.

Enforcing a Vendor SLA through Penalties

Now let's look at motivating factors behind penalties. A vendor may be quicker to issue a check for a credit or scribble a discount on a future bill than they are to spend the time to fix the root cause of a problem. As the internal point person, your job will be managing the different agendas within your organization. While the CFO may be pleased with reduction in future outsourcing fees, a front-line manager who is receiving poor service and will not personally

Escalation

While constantly calling the president of your outsourcing vendor about SLA issues that could have been rectified with your primary contacts does not help your business relationship, having access to the vendor's senior management is a sound strategy for handling escalating unresolved problems. The key here is to set up the escalation policy with the identification of time and severity triggers that would constitute bumping up accountability to a higher level. Your vendor may already have a structure like this in place and it may be merely a matter of educating you about whom to call and when. Ideally, the vendor will have a clear escalation policy and structure in place and you won't have to call anyone: they'll call you because the matter has escalated internally based on their own rules. Having the appropriate names and phone numbers in advance is a prudent strategy, though.

Have Reasonable Service Level Guarantees

It is important to look at how reasonable and realistic an SLA is, and consider the guarantees you're requesting as well. There are few key questions you can ask to ascertain whether a service level guarantee is reasonable or not:

- Can the service provider really achieve this?
- What is the supportive evidence?
  - Have they done it for another customer?
  - Do they have a history of it in your organization?
  - If they have done it in a similar area, will the same necessarily hold true for this new service?
- Do you believe they can achieve what they promise, and make a profit?
- Do you believe they can maintain what they promise on an ongoing basis?

Ultimately, if the service levels are not realistic, they will cast a shadow of unrealistic expectations on the agreement, which can cause friction between the customer and the vendor—or set a precedent of leniency that seeps into other service areas as well.

SLAs: Complexity vs. Effectiveness

Having a Service Level Agreement that encompasses dozens and dozens of pages doesn't guarantee good service. It is important to step back and look at the SLA and ask yourself if it is going to be a headache to administer and enforce, or if it's a real tool that will improve service levels.

Remember: Service level management must link SLA metrics with *business goals.*

Internal SLAs in Human Resources

Wal-Mart's internal customer service standards
reminded me of the philosophy of the Three Musketeers,
"It's all for one and one for all"!

(Michael Bergdahl, former executive, Wal-Mart)

As HR outsourcing continues to rise, Service Level Agreements become more and more prevalent to manage the relationship between the service providers and customers. As this paradigm flourishes between external vendors and their customers, it begs the question of why internal HR departments cannot extend something like this to their internal customers.

From a sheer aspect of survival, HR professionals need to take a careful look at the shift toward outsourcing providers and how aspects of that model can be applied internally. As the outsourcing model takes hold as a primary means of fulfilling HR's work, the work that remains in HR is coming under increased scrutiny. The service quality and return on investment of these activities is already being closely compared to and examined against the outsourced activities. The question arises as to why the remaining activities cannot be outsourced as well.

There certainly are aspects of the structure of an outsourcing organization that an internal HR department will not be able to duplicate. Nor is this just a simple exercise of mimicking.

Resistance vs. Benefits of SLAs

Why HR May be Resistant to SLAs

Many HR professionals are not quick to adopt the SLA approach and apply it to their own activities, and to subsequently be judged by their internal customers. There are many reasons why:

- Fear of exposure of poor service level quality on the part of HR
- Fear that this information will be used in the case for outsourcing HR
- A lack of understanding in measuring the quality of service for HR's services
- A resistance to spend precious resources on an additional set of metrics that must be managed by HR.

Benefits of Internal SLAs

On the other hand, there are several benefits to implementing internal SLAs:

- Clarifying requirements and responsibilities
- Educating customers on the process
- Identifying ways to measure success
- Clarifying resource limitations
- Giving internal customers options.

Clarifying Requirements and Responsibilities

At a basic level, understanding the customer requirements and the roles and responsibilities that all parties will play in the process is critical to the success of an SLA, and all of these components need to be addressed up front. Internal SLAs use more common language than external SLAs, which are normally crafted within more of a legal and contractual context. The internal SLA is a means for memorializing agreement, and is not a document from which litigation can potentially arise.

Educating Customers on the Process

A failure to meet customer expectations often results from the misperceptions by a customer who does not really understand how the process works. The responsibility for this lies with HR, as the service provider, to educate internal customers about what the service will normally look like in terms of time, service levels, and other factors.

During this period of understanding, the customer has the opportunity to either realign their expectations or negotiate for different levels of services to suit their needs.

Identifying Ways to Measure Success

How successfully have you identified the critical components of managing the relationship? If the scorecard is not agreed upon, the likelihood that both parties will be operating from the same perspective is unlikely. This sets up a paradigm for failure.

Clarifying Resource Limitations

HR, like any department, has a budget and financial resources. Peaks and valleys of demand are clearly affected by its financial resources. External departments need to understand that.

Giving Internal Customers Options

After internal departments are given an understanding of HR department resources, possible solutions can be created. This can open the relationship to negotiation. Rather than simply saying "no" to a customer request because of finite resources, HR can put a dollar amount on the customer's request and test the level of need of the customer. How many of the customers *really* need this? Is the department willing to put up part of their own budget to satisfy these requirements? By having clear service levels, and giving the option of additional service at additional cost, both parties can be served. This also helps mitigate the intrusion of a negative tone into the relationship with the internal customers, because they can take certain requirements off the table if they are unwilling or unable to pay for them.

Key Things to Consider When Implementing Internal SLAs in HR

- Use internal SLAs to improve understanding of costs and resources allocation
- Use internal SLAs to manage the scope of HR's duties
- Use internal SLAs to better track volume and report on HR activities
- Approach HR department penalties and incentives carefully
- Ease into internal SLAs and build your SLA muscles.

Use Internal SLAs to Improve Understanding of Costs and Resources Allocation

By having a better handle on workload and resources that are tied to service levels, HR can take more of an active role in effectively managing resources. When a particular area of the business is consuming a larger than normal part of HR's resources, proactive steps should be taken.

Most HR departments do not allocate internal charges to other departments for their services. The measurement and reporting of workload is often an area that is not effectively reported by HR. The volume of transactions, such as last month's transactions and anticipated transactions for the current month, need to be articulated and tied to historical frames of reference (transactions recorded at the same time last year, etc.).

By carefully monitoring resources that are effectively tied to Service Level Agreements, HR be will be able to understand and gauge its ability to meet customer needs based on existing resources. Without this, there is simply the continued pressure to do more with less, which is the way things have most often happened in the past. A documented paper trail is what usually has been lacking on the part of a HR to prove their case and to demonstrate the business case for additional resources.

Understanding resource usage allows for better accountability and will mean that HR is not left holding the bag. For example, because there is unusually high turnover within a certain department that eats up resources needed for normal turnover within other departments, a business case can be made for some sort of charge-back to the department with the unusually high needs.

The goal of resources allocation is not to refuse service or justify diminished levels of service to internal customers; resources allocation is meant to be used as a management tool and as a quantification of reality versus plan. This will allow senior management better visibility of what is taking place, and it will also allow them to make adjustments accordingly.

Use Internal SLAs to Manage the Scope of HR's Duties

A problem with the internal service relationship is that, in many circumstances, exceptions are made to the scope of work in the spirit of teamwork and internal accommodation. While an external vendor may go that extra mile to make the customer happy or will simply charge for the extra service, an internal service provider may be required to fulfill duties that are outside their normal areas and levels of service in the spirit of shouldering in and being a team player.

In project management, this is called *scope creep,* and it is something that must be carefully managed to make sure that primary objectives do not suffer at the expense of efforts directed to other activities. A balance must be struck between HR's flexibility with regard to day-to-day changing needs in the organization, and HR's need to remain focused on its primary objectives.

Use Internal SLAs to Better Track Volume and Report on HR Activities

Reporting on Service Level Agreements is one of the biggest challenges on the horizon for HR professionals. Since many HR processes are not fully automated, tracking information is not as easy as in the IT department, for example.

Bearing that in mind, HR can look to these other functional areas of the business to benchmark and find practices that can be adapted to HR's part of the business.

Trouble tickets are a model that is used in IT and other functional areas to log, identify, and track to resolution issues that come up. This can be a useful tool for HR for identifying trends and fixes that relate to commonly occurring problems, and it is also a way to account for the endless amount of time that is spent by HR staff in "putting out fires" throughout the day. By logging these activities, it can give insight into how much effort is being expended to deal with issues, and this can be used in the case for outsourcing, in the investment in a solution to a problem, or even for the need for additional head count!

Except in large organizations, where HR call centers are more prevalent, effective tracking of interactions between HR and its customers is not common. That is to say, calls with benefits questions, for example, are dealt with but often not recorded and tied to employee records or other HR personnel logs. Most HRIS systems have the ability to utilize a notes feature, but this is often not taken advantage of in ways like this.

The Customer Relationship Management model (CRM) is one from which HR can learn many lessons; having transaction history and notes provide a record of continuity within the HR department by allowing any staff member visibility of the actions and conversations that have already taken place. In turn, the customer is relieved of having to bring a new person they are speaking with up to speed. This seems inherently professional, yet it is often an area that is overlooked in HR, as individual staff members most often try to rely on their own memory and the likelihood that they will be dealing with the same customer themselves. This, of course, is a poor foundation for organizational knowledge management of customer issues and necessitates the tracking down of relevant information, which creates delays and more opportunities for the degradation of the historical facts.

Approach HR Department Penalties and Incentives Carefully

Just as there must be penalties for poor performance in an SLA with an external vendor, there must be incentives to guarantee and motivate in the case of internal SLAs in HR. This could be an internal budget charge-back, transfer, or other remediation that will be taken seriously (i.e., penalizing HR's budget a certain dollar amount that is withdrawn or even transferred to the budget of the department receiving the poor service).

This is certainly not a concept that would be normally well received by HR. Despite this, it is a viable way to hold HR to task on its performance. If an outsourcing provider can be held accountable for reasonable service level targets and penalized financially if these are not met, why can't an internal HR department, with a budget, function under a similar paradigm? The answer most HR professionals would give is that the outsourcing provider is operating with a profit margin and HR barely has sufficient budget to function. The logic in this needs further scrutiny. If the outsourcing provider can perform these services and add a profit after covering expenses, the question must be posed as to why HR can't provide close to that level of service, without profit added on. In light of factors such as economies of scale, inexpensive offshore labor, and scalable technology, this is, perhaps, an oversimplification of the issue, but I believe it is a view to carefully consider.

This brings the discussion back to the concepts of basic behavioral psychology. We've looked at penalties and incentives (punishment and rewards) for external vendors, and how these, when applied internally, must be done with equal rigor. However, by assessing penalties against the HR department in the form of budget charge-backs or something along that order, the ability to sustain service levels may be compromised, so this must be monitored meticulously. Unlike an outsourcing vendor, HR does not have a profit level factored in—and HR budgets are not known to be fat with lots of dollars built-in that could act as a buffer.

Just as I mentioned that penalties assessed against an external vendor need not always be financial, non-monetary penalties can also be applied internally to the HR department. Again, remember that you are trying to drive behavior. That might be accomplished by exacting leverage upon those in management and leadership roles within HR. For example, while reducing the bonus of an HR executive for not meeting service levels may be utilized, forcing them to go before senior management (or even the board) to present and explain the missed service levels is something they would probably actively avoid.

Incentives are the other side of the equation and should be crafted in a way that rewards the contributions of those involved in a tangible way. This can take the form of bonuses to HR managers, and possibly a team bonus that is included in the bonus structure of individual HR employees in addition to their own performance reviews and incentive structure.

Ease into Internal SLAs—and Build Your SLA Muscles!

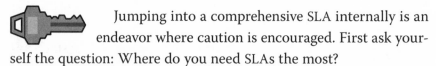 Jumping into a comprehensive SLA internally is an endeavor where caution is encouraged. First ask yourself the question: Where do you need SLAs the most?

Start with identifying one to three internal HR services that are good candidates for Service Level Management. Within each service, identify one or two critical metrics tied to customer-perceived service levels.

If these metrics have not been gathered in the past, it is probably prudent to track them internally for a certain period of time to get an idea of what the potential service level targets might be—instead of picking arbitrary target levels and engaging the customer with optimistic targets that have no history of being achievable.

It is important to pilot an internal SLA before these are rolled up to the whole organization. This will give HR an understanding of what works and what doesn't, and what service levels it is comfortable achieving.

Piloting an SLA program with a department or business unit with which HR already has a positive relationship will give HR an opportunity to learn as it goes. This process will allow achievable performance levels to be identified, and measurements and reporting tools to be refined.

Service Standards in HR

While HR may not be ready to move toward full-blown Service Level Agreements, it must begin to set internal service standards. These standards can be used initially as a target or guide within the HR department to set goals for service level improvement and the reduction in service variation.

These initial standards are also a way to collect historical data—because jumping into an SLA without having historical data to back up your ability to deliver on a promise is a disservice to all parties involved. While well intended, it can lead to distrust in HR's ability, and this may be difficult to regain later on.

By taking the opportunity to grow into and understand their own service standards, HR will become more comfortable with strengthening their commitment to written SLAs.

 KEY THOUGHTS

Internal SLAs in HR

- HR managers may not see the immediate benefits of internal SLAs. They also may have concerns about how to go about implementing, negotiating, and satisfying SLAs. The benefits of internal SLAs to HR include:
  - Improved relationship with customers
  - Better leverage in budget negotiations

- Improved ability to compete with outsourcing vendors.
- Internal SLAs should:
  - Define required performance levels
  - Set and manage customer expectations
  - Assign responsibility and roles
  - Measure customer satisfaction
  - Map resources to needed services.
- Without careful preparation, HR may find their Service Level Agreements being turned against them, as business units use them as documentation to cover their own departmental errors, or to circumvent policy.
- Carefully consider whether an internal SLA is something for which return on investment can be shown. Check to be sure that budget expenditures in time and resources demonstrate some quantifiable positive return.

15

ROI AND
THE HR FUNCTION

*No other investment yields as great a return as the investment
in education. An educated workforce is the foundation of
every community and the future of every economy.*

(Brad Henry, Governor, State of Oklahoma)

FOR many years, HR was simply not viewed as a department or function that contributed to the bottom line, and in many organizations it still isn't. HR is often considered necessary *overhead* and it is a common management perception that the only way it contributes to the bottom line is by keeping the cost of HR operations low. If we as HR professionals are going to address this paradigm and look at return on investment, we need to closely examine HR's value to the organization, its contribution to the bottom line, and how improvements and investments in HR will yield increased financial results.

In doing so, we must establish HR as part of the *value chain.*

What is that?

Your company, as with all companies, creates some kind of value. That is why it is in business. The HR department needs to create value through its processes. That is why it exists.

So how do we define *value*? Value can be demonstrated in the following equation which shows the ratio of the worth of an activity (HR Service) to its cost.

$$\text{Value} = \frac{Worth}{Cost}$$

So HR activities must have some worth to the organization that outweigh the cost to the organization. This attacks the notion of "necessary overhead," and it is critical in demonstrating the return on investment (ROI) for HR.

The Cost of Quality in HR

As we focus on ROI in HR, we need to look at the negative side of the equation: What is poor HR service and poor quality costing the organization?

There are many ways that poor service in the HR department can be quite costly to an organization, but the defects are not always obvious. If HR was a manufacturing line, there would be a big pile of circuit boards, toasters, or other flawed product "output" that would have to be refurbished, recycled, or hauled away because it was waste. Beyond the cost of the raw materials and the labor, there would be costs to store or dispose of this waste. So what are parallel costs in HR? How about:

- The cost of third-party recruiting fees, because hiring managers don't like the performance of the internal recruiting efforts?

- The cost of workers' compensation premiums from poorly handled claims?

- The cost of diminished productivity from bureaucratic HR processes?

Accurate Assessment of Costs

In calculating return on investment in HR, it is critical to accurately assess the investment part of the equation, and that means accurately gauging total costs. In Information Technology circles there is a concept known as Total Cost of Ownership (TCO), which takes into account training, ongoing support, network and communication costs, and other expenses—in addition to what would be considered the primary investment.

This thinking can be applied to any project by remembering that the initial investment may not be representative of what a project will necessarily require over its life cycle. See Figure 15-1 following.

Investment Cost Model

Online Resource Center	Available in the Online Resource Center	Life Cycle of Project, Initiative, or Technology		
		Initial/ Acquisition	Operation	Growth & Change
Resources	Labor			
	Training/Support			
	Materials			
	Facilities			
	Vendor Services			
	Hardware			
	Software			
	Network & Communication			

FIGURE 15-1

Straight to the Bottom Line

It is important to consider the relevance to profitability that savings (lowering expenses) make. Salespeople are often revered because they bring in revenue and that is what sustains the business, right? No. *Profit* is what sustains the business.

$$Profit = Revenue - Expenses.$$

So improvements in either of these two areas (increasing profit or lowering expenses) will drive revenue. Most of the improvements that HR will make in their operations will be around lowering expenses.

So, let's look at an example:

If your company spends $2,200 per employee a year on training, benefits, and other HR administration, and you have 500 employees, that equals $1,100,000 in expenses. By reducing this by 5%, it generates a savings of about $55,000.

Now, HR does not get viewed in the same way as sales because HR has always been viewed as "overhead" and a cost center, rather than as revenue generating.

Profit margins vary by industry, but let's say your company operates at a 5% Net Profit Margin (Revenue minus Expenses). By saving just $50,000 in a year (roughly $4,200/month), that is the rough equivalent of a salesperson bringing in $1,000,000 worth of revenue. The point is that this money goes straight to the bottom line and equals pure profit.

Would it be worth dedicating at least part of someone's time in HR to help drive those savings?

Quantifying ROI

Return on investment is difficult to quantify in many of the things that HR does. Despite this, HR must be relentless in attempting to measure and demonstrate the value of HR's activities. This pressure comes from C-level management (CEO, CFO, etc.) who must continue to answer to the shareholders, investors, and/or owners who want them to *"Show me the money!"* Even programs with cultural significance such as family-friendly programs (Employee Assistance Programs, flexible schedules, and dependent care spending accounts) need to demonstrate their value to the organization. This can be exceedingly tricky, but the onus falls on HR.

As we as HR professionals begin to look at programs that are difficult to quantify directly, we must draw clear correlations to other things that *can* be quantified. Using our family-friendly program example, tying these programs to lower absenteeism or lower turnover may be the linkage that can then be quantified into hard dollar savings.

However, you must make sure to have a solid correlation between the family-friendly programs and lower turnover—and not just a coincidental correlation or one that you *hope* exists.

(See the Maiden and the Volcano, chapter 1, page 27.)

Hard Dollars

In defining what hard dollars are, the key is that the savings are tangible—meaning they are measurable and quantifiable. What some consider to be hard-dollar savings differs depending on to whom you are talking. As stated earlier, some organizations do not consider time savings unless they are subsequently converted into tangible savings in labor costs.

Clearly, dollar savings that are directly reflected in recruiting budgets are considered hard-dollar savings. For example, money that was budgeted for relocation that was not used because of improved processes would be considered a hard-dollar savings.

Soft Dollars

Not all benefits are as clear as those covered under hard-dollar savings. When service levels are improved or, sometimes, when additional expenses are *not* accrued (e.g., not having to pay overtime), these are considered what are called *soft dollars*. These initially intangible elements often comprise a great deal of most process-improvement efforts: improved customer service, reduced stress from work, fewer mistakes that have to be corrected, and all of the other benefits that cascade into every area of an organization.

While the qualitative aspect of recruiting is very important, the challenge of HR recruiters is to try to translate soft-dollar savings into hard-dollar savings. For example, speeding up the time to hire a salesperson can be translated into revenue from the quota that salesperson will generate. Those are hard dollars, and are what your CEO will take note of and see value in.

"Show Me the Money!"

Demonstrating the ROI of HR Improvement Efforts

Much has been said about the danger of assumptions. Therefore, assuming that senior management clearly understands the value of the work you do in HR is a dangerous endeavor. It is the job of your department to really sell the value that HR is bringing to the organization.

To demonstrate the ROI of your efforts, it is increasingly necessary to effectively collect data, analyze it, and prove your case. This should include involving your CFO or controller by eliciting their input in helping to define the scorecard they will use to judge your efforts. They should clarify what they will view as hard and soft savings, and provide you baselines of improvements that they will take note of or even be impressed by.

A colleague of mine once pointed out that her organization's executive management did not count savings in time created through process improvement unless it could be shown as a reduction in head count.

That is to say, saving a recruiter an hour a day through some kind of process improvement was not assumed to mean that the recruiter was putting that time savings into other value-added activities and doing a better job recruiting. Unless it was quite obvious that labor costs were going down or recruiter efficiency ratios were going up, the savings was "hypothetical" in the eyes of senior management—in other words, the savings didn't exist.

This is the hard-line business approach that most C-level executives take in viewing the ROI of their HR department's operations. ROI impacts their profit and loss statements and, though the qualitative aspects of HR are something that smart executives are mindful of, your efforts are often considered administrative rather than strategic.

If HR is to become a strategic player in the organization, it is necessary for you to make the case with both hard- and soft-dollar examples of savings, and with a clear demonstration of an ever-increasing return on investment.

The Past, Present, and Future: A Case for ROI

Just like the three Ghosts of Past, Present, and Future in Charles Dickens' *A Christmas Carol,* think about where you have been, where you currently stand, and where you are going to be in the future regarding your HR operations. In order to demonstrate a solid case for senior management, you may need to walk them through how things have been done in the past and how they are being done now. While none of us want to point out how much time and money we have wasted in the past, looking at it in order to build an effective and persuasive case for change can be very beneficial.

After showing what has happened in the past and bringing things up to the present, you can systematically and straightforwardly project what the employee benefits function, for example, will look like if you don't make certain changes now. What will the costs be in one year? Two years? Five years?

This is the type of case that must be made to justify improvements and investment in areas such as improved technology. For example, how much time will be saved through better stock option administration software? Do you know? Can you estimate this? Can you articulate the savings? Can you show how much time was wasted using the existing methods, and how that will be improved?

While predicting future savings can be considered guesswork, your predictions will be taken more seriously the better you are equipped to support them with historical and current data. In addition, being fluid about future time savings can demonstrate your understanding of the unknown elements that can impact projected efficiency. With that in mind, future savings can be given as a range, with a conservative to optimistic scope.

Some Perspective about ROI

It is important to think about the true meaning of return on investment, that is, what you *actually* get in return on the investment. The point here is that calculating ROI in advance is an exercise and only a hypothesis—*what actually happens is the real ROI.*

Unfortunately, most organizations use ROI as an analytical tool to build a business case for something they are going to do, or are thinking about doing—but they rarely go back and gauge ROI for things that have been done. The cost/benefit analysis is definitely important to make informed business decisions, but these decisions need to be checked and validated later on. Why? *To make better decisions in the future.*

ROI calculation can be an almost completely fictional exercise, where costs are not accurately accounted for and benefits are over-estimated. This may not be attributable to deception or ignorance, but merely to optimism. As you become more adept at improving HR operations, you will begin to understand the challenges of change management, the unforeseen costs that you will instinctively pad into your estimated budgets, and the wisdom of presenting a more conservative and balanced estimation of your success. While it is important to present a convincing cost/benefit analysis, there is strategic value in under-promising and over-delivering.

The challenge may lie in an organizational threshold that the senior executives set for ROI, which means that projects are only given approval if they hit a minimum percentage of return (e.g., 15%, 25%, or 50%). This is a common driver of ROI estimates which are often constructed to simply meet or beat this threshold.

Until the benefits of a project have ended, ROI is an ongoing equation to be followed as a journey and not a destination. By monitoring and learning over time how to increase the ROI value gained from a project, you can successfully apply this improved understanding to the management of other improvement projects in the future.

KEY THOUGHTS

- Whether proving the quality of your current work or making a pitch for investment in the future, it is important to build a solid case with clear data that speaks to the hard-dollar needs of senior management.
- It can be incredibly difficult to turn everything into hard-dollar savings, but HR must strive to do this. If soft-dollar benefits such as improved customer service levels can subsequently be measured in terms of qualitative data, it can only help the case for return on investment that will satisfy the C-suite.

Maintaining
Excellence

The journey toward excellence is a never-ending road.
Some people, because they see no end to their road,
never take the first step.

(H. James Harrington, CEO, Harrington Institute, Inc.)

TAKE the first step! Although the benefits of process improvements are rarely earned in the short term, your return on investment will be gained over time by *sustaining* improvements that lead to *continued* savings. To ensure this, any improvements made should be monitored at regular intervals. This also holds true for outsourcing initiatives as well as the investment in technology.

Unfortunately, as most organizations move on to new projects, their focus travels elsewhere. This constant shifting and changing is a natural part of an organization's growth and fluidity. Despite this, a concerted effort on your part must be made to revisit past projects in order to assess their current state and to make any adjustments to ensure continued benefits.

The following are some key recommendations to follow as projects get completed:

Conduct a *Project Postmortem*

 After each project is completed and the results are communicated, controls are put in place, and discus-

197

sion of the next project has begun, it is important to assess how the finished project went. And not just what the results were, but what can be learned from the project to improve future projects.

The *planned vs. actual performance of the project* as an activity should be gauged in key areas including:

- Goals
- Schedule
- Quality
- Budget.

The project team should be assessed on:

- Team member selection and participation
- Project selection and planning
- Meetings and communication
- Team responsibilities and management of the project.

Three other key questions need to be asked:

- What went right?
- What went wrong?
- What recommendations does the team have for the future?

By answering these questions and spending a little more time at the end of the project, your learning and experience in project management will be greatly enhanced, and you will be that much more confident and prepared for the next project.

Have Sufficient Project Documentation

Individual staff members will move in and out of an organization and it is not uncommon to have all of the members of a project team gone within a year or two. They may not all quit; however, some will be laid off, some may be assigned to other parts of the company, or transferred to another region, or any number of possible reasons that will make them unavailable or unable to contribute to revisiting a particular project.

The only way to preserve the organization's knowledge and memory of a particular project is to have excellent documentation. This allows a project to continue to be a viable entity within the organization, and to have longevity, living on to serve the organization long after the individual team members have moved on.

It is important to keep:

- Team charters (along with a list of team members)
- Raw and analyzed data
- Notes, findings, and recommendations
- Decisions that were made by the organization, and any supporting documentation and reasoning (e.g., why one outsourcing provider was chosen over another)
- Projected savings and future benefits to the organization
- A timeline for future meetings to assess a project's continued contribution to the organization
- Naming someone accountable for future project results.

Set Firm Future Calendar Dates for Project Reviews

The project team should make recommendations for regular assessments to review and reassess the project over time. Once these dates are agreed upon, they must be set as firm calendar dates. This could, for example, be a schedule of three months out, six months out, and one and two years out.

To accomplish this, the specific people or roles within the organization (CFO, VP of HR, IT Director, etc.) must be engaged, and someone must be in charge of making this happen. In the age of email and electronic calendars, it is feasible to set dates well in advance and put these on people's schedules even at distant increments. The specific dates are not as important as it is to make sure that these meetings simply take place around the timed intervals that were agreed upon—so that they cannot be ignored or collectively forgotten.

The ongoing effort to improve HR operations should also include a multitude of smaller projects that have already taken place. Regularly revisiting and assessing the projects can be accomplished by grouping the assessments together. This can be accomplished through monthly or quarterly HR excellence meetings that include regular assessments of HR's performance. But however it is done, time must be set aside to go back and look at what has been accomplished, and to make adjustments for the future.

Ensure Accountability by the Process Owner

While encouraging accountability, it is not advisable to make the whole team responsible for the future success of the project. As stated earlier, at some point all of the team members may have moved on. Despite this, if the *buck doesn't stop somewhere*, chances are nobody will rush to fill this role.

So who does?

If improvements are to be maintained and if they are to have some sort of sustainable financial impact on the company, the person who has budget or profit and loss responsibility for that process would be the most likely person to be held accountable that improvements continue—or, at the least, that efforts are made to move in that direction if things have gone off course. This might be the HR Manager, Director, or the supervisor of a particular function such as benefits, recruitment, or training.

As a result, that *role or office*, not necessarily a specific person, would hold responsibility for project benefits and ROI. Therefore, if a new HR manager comes in, that person would now be tasked with maintaining the improved process levels. This could be accomplished with a line item on a performance review, or recorded in some other place to tie this to the duties and responsibilities of the current process owner. In line with tying this to a performance review, bonuses or incentives could be tied to sustained improvements.

In any case, it is imperative that some plan is put in place that will ensure ownership of the organizational benefits that the project team worked so hard to create. There is always some way to accomplish this, and a diligent effort must be made to ensure this accountability. If it is reasonable to say that this area of performance falls within a person's domain, he or she needs to be tasked with maintaining improvements—whether that entails revisiting the old project to find out where any disconnect may have taken place, or to commence on a new process-improvement effort to address the existing issue.

If you are the person I'm alluding to, the one who would be considered the process owner (and that would make sense, since you are reading this book!), then this is the moment of truth where you need to demonstrate your commitment to *HR Excellence.* Remember, *excellence* is not accomplished in a single event; it is a continuous and cumulative activity. The significant ROI from most process improvements comes from sustaining and accruing benefits over time.

Encourage a Culture of Excellence

The most important part of sustaining improvements and guaranteeing ongoing success is to encourage a culture of excellence within your HR department. Cultural changes are very difficult to instill, but it is something the HR department and all of us as HR professionals must strive to do.

A critical part of selecting the proper team is involving the people who not only have the technical skills to work on improvement projects, but who also believe strongly in the concept of constant improvement, and in the assurance that their work will make a difference. These individuals are critical as spokespeople for your efforts and will evangelize what is being done within the HR department and throughout the rest of the company.

The Alarm Clock Question

Getting people to care about HR excellence comes from addressing a basic motivational question: "What do *I* get out of all of this HR excellence stuff?"

When an employee wakes up in the morning, s/he probably doesn't think about how s/he can achieve service excellence or have zero defects. S/he thinks about the things that will improve the quality of his or her work life and his or her own career, such as:

"How can I avoid having to put out fires all day?"

"How can I get my boss off my back?"

"How can I get the line-managers to do X, Y and Z?"

"How can I stop the phone from ringing with unnecessary requests?"

"How can I get to work on more meaningful projects that are interesting (will build my skills, will help me understand busi-ness-line functions better, will help get me promoted, etc.)?"

If you are the HR leader in your organization, then the culture of *HR Excellence* begins with you. You must be its inspiration, its galvanizing force, its motivation, its champion, and its succession planner! The culture of excellence must be sustained, and it must become part of ongoing HR operations.

 KEY THOUGHTS

- Utilize the end of the project as a chance to recap what took place and to make recommendations for future projects.
- If the organization believes enough in the merits of a project to create a team and invest other resources, it should be prepared to put controls in place to gauge ongoing results and accountability to ensure continuing commitment to excellence.
- HR excellence does not start and end with a single project or even a string of projects. It must become a part of the culture in HR.

So what do we do? Anything. Something.
So long as we just don't sit there. If we screw it up, start over.
Try something else. If we wait until we've satisfied
all the uncertainties, it may be too late.

(Lee Iacocca, former CEO, Chrysler Corporation)

CONCLUSION

With enough understanding of your processes and your customers, you can begin to look at the measurements and come up with some deeper analysis to help you craft improvements. This begins with understanding the cause-and-effect relationships between the input variables and the output or outcomes within the processes.

By utilizing graphical and statistical tools, you will be better able to understand patterns and trends that will lead you toward effective sustainable improvements.

THE *NEW* HR MANDATES

CONCLUSION

Now you have come to the end of this discussion. I hope you are excited about starting to apply the concepts you have learned!

As you have seen, there is no single solution or perfect system for improving HR operations (or any other type of operations), but you now have a framework from which to view process-improvement efforts more holistically. You can enhance this with deeper study of the concepts presented in this book.

If you now want more information, this is a good sign. This book is meant as a primer for the continued development of your skills within the evolving world of HR.

As the outsourcing trend continues, and as HR becomes an increasingly significant component of global operations, a new landscape is unfolding before the HR professional. As discussed at the beginning of this book, the management imperative is that HR must become more of a *strategic partner* in business.

In *HR Excellence,* I have pulled together answers to questions HR needs to address, as well as successful approaches from other functional areas within the organization, which I have translated and condensed into an HR context. The following chart presents what I call "The *New* HR Mandate," and it summarizes the key concepts covered in this book.

The *New* HR Mandates: Key Concepts Covered in *HR Excellence*

- HR must be more strategic, but, as HR moves to a more strategic role, it must *first* effectively and efficiently manage transactional HR operations.

- HR must continuously and methodically gather Voice of the Customer information and focus HR operations based on customer requirements (explicit and implicit).

- HR metrics and analytics must grow beyond simple metrics that involve only counting, basic percentages, and averages: HR must gather more qualitative data and utilize statistical analysis and other tools to improve operations and utilize the information to improve forward-looking decisions, and not just function as a historical reporting mechanism.

- Causal analysis is critical for HR to understand "what levers must be pulled" to drive performance metrics and improve HR operations.

- Outsourcing is an oversimplified answer to HR problems at most organizations: You cannot outsource a mess, or something that you don't understand, and expect success in HR—nor can you outsource parts of or all of HR and expect success without devoting sufficient internal resources to effectively source for and then manage the outsourcing arrangement.

- Service Level Management and Service Level Agreements are critical to effectively manage an outsourcing arrangement and are ideal to be used internally between HR and its internal customers to demonstrate HR's success and to manage internal customer expectations.

- Return on investment in HR must be recognized and quantified in hard-dollar savings. This is the way the CEO and CFO see the business, and improvements in HR must ultimately translate into positive bottom-line results. *It is the responsibility of HR to connect the dots on the ROI of HR activities, and not the CFO's.*

CONCLUDING REMARKS

Whether you are the chief HR officer in your organization, or you simply want to build and expand upon your HR knowledge, this book has been designed to help you improve the performance of your HR operations, and allow you to contribute more significantly to strategic activities throughout your organization.

The Online Resource Center will grow over time, so check back frequently for suggested reading and links to useful articles and tools. If you have not already done so, see the Introduction for instructions on how to access the Online Resource Center.

I truly welcome feedback about *HR Excellence* and I look forward to your comments about those areas where you would like to see additional information, future training, and online learning provided.

Please contact me directly at comments@hrexcellence.net.

Appendix A

Advanced Tools

Be Not Afraid!

This section might scare some of you away. That is why it was moved to the Appendix.

If these advanced tools were really your cup of tea, you'd probably be engineers or scientists . . . not HR professionals. Don't worry, though, if some of this is outside your comfort zone; it's helpful to at least know about these tools. Should the need arise, you can learn more about them, or find someone already knowledgeable to apply the information for you, in order to accomplish an objective or make business decisions based on facts rather than intuition.

The larger your organization, the more likely these tools will be worth the extra effort to review and utilize. Don't hesitate to get help, since engaging outside help may be much more efficient than going through the full learning curve on your own.

What you need to understand at this point is that these tools exist and are available. Their function is to systematically identify root causes that will enable you to make decisions based on facts.

The following is an overview of some of the more advanced statistical and causal analysis tools available today to more closely identify the root cause of certain effects, such as variation, so that these can be controlled to a certain degree.

As we look at causal analysis, it is important to remember that the focus needs to be on *proving* hypotheses about our processes. That is to say, having a hypothesis about a process issue is not enough. We must be able to systematically prove it in a manner that is logical and reliable.

All of the tools that were listed in chapters 7 and 8 come with enough instruction in the text and the Online Resource Center to start applying them immediately. But the advanced tools are just that: *advanced.* I will look at some of these tools and briefly show how they might be applied in HR.

I will cover:

- Data Mean and Standard Deviation

- Analysis of Variation (ANOVA)

- Regression Analysis

- Design of Experiments (DOE)

- Failure Mode and Effects Analysis (FMEA)

Data Mean and Standard Deviation

The *mean* of the data is simply the average (for example, the average hiring time for engineering positions was 47 days). This calculation is commonly used in HR.

The next step is to calculate the *standard deviation,* which shows the variation of data in a process. This calculation is *rarely* done in HR. Using our hiring time example (mean or average = 47 days), it could tell us that *the standard deviation* (variation) *was 17 days.* That shows that the majority of hires were within 17 days (+ or -) of the average. Therefore, it shows that almost all of the hires happened within 30 and 64 days (47 − 17 = 30 and 47 + 17 = 64).

Understanding this variation helps us to understand and focus-in on processes that have a lot of variation.

So what is *a lot* of variation? Let's look at the next tool.

Analysis of Variation (ANOVA)

Analysis of Variation (ANOVA) is a statistical test of different sets of data to determine whether variation in measures has an impact on process outputs. ANOVA establishes a level of confidence in whether variations are tied to a particular factor or can be explained by random chance or natural variation. In other words, are the differences in these numbers due to some factor or not?

For example, the question of varying lengths of hiring cycle times could be looked at and explored in terms of whether the variation in them was significant. If the hiring times were all within a day or two of 47 days (+ or − 2 days, instead of 17), there might not be much reason for the difference. If there is a big difference, this might be tied to something, and how significant this is could be expressed as a confidence percent, i.e., "We are 95% confident that having an initial job requirements meeting between the recruiter and the hiring manager on engineering jobs reduces the time to hire."

Optimization with Multiple Variables

Trying to analyze and understand the causal relationship between variables becomes increasing difficult when multiple variables are present, as you try to isolate and understand each one. Scatter plots show the relationship between two variables, but there are rarely only two variables to be understood.

When looking at the individual parameters of a process, many organizations try to adjust *One Factor at a Time* (OFAT) in an effort to understand relationships to process outcomes. This doesn't take into account the interaction among factors and how combinations of factors can produce different outcomes. Testing one factor at a time has many drawbacks in that the results are: 1) often unreliable, 2) many experiments are required (which can be cost-prohibitive), and 3) they fail to take into account the interaction or dependency between different variables.

Regression Analysis

Regression analysis allows us to learn more about the relationship between several independent (predictor) variables and a dependent (criterion) variable. It takes historical data and creates a mathematical model that can be extrapolated and used to predict how the process will respond in the future. In essence this helps us understand what lever or combination of levers we need to pull to create the effect we want and to drive the process in the direction we desire.

A strategic organizational project which utilizes regression analysis could be the analysis of employee turnover. While rankings from different studies continue to surface about what the key causes of turnover are, there are rarely singular, isolated causes. Rather, combinations of factors influence turnover. There have been many studies that examine turnover and look at multiple factors through the use of regression analysis.

Design of Experiments (DOE)

The concept of Design of Experiments (DOE) addresses the problem of the many different variables (or factors) which play a part in the outcome of a process. More specifically, these are called process parameters (factors) which are analyzed to estimate their effect on process outcomes (response).

Compared to the basic tools discussed in earlier chapters, this is a more complex approach to improving processes. While a small organization may also benefit from this approach, a large organization would be the most likely user. Though there is a learning curve to utilize this approach and specialized software will probably be needed, the benefits from Design of Experiments can provide significant return on investment of the time and money involved.

Design of Experiments is a systematic approach that looks at all factors simultaneously. By creating a mathematical model, we can provide information about how the system works, including the interaction among factors, by looking at various combinations to identify an optimum solution.

Many organizations are looking for ways to optimize their employer referral programs. This is a good example for Design of Experiments. Rather than simply varying the dollar amount (one factor at a time) to figure out what the best dollar amount is, the many different factors can be looked at simultaneously.

So how can we identify the different factors that influence the optimal result? Depending on what is known already about the employee referral program success, the list may have already been narrowed down to a handful of items. If not, screening designs can be created to help whittle down the many different factors that influence optimization and to remove those that really have no impact. Once the group of factors that matter have been identified, the next step is to gather data and optimize them. This can be done by experimenting for a few months with the employee referral program through different approaches, such as contests and promotions that vary from month to month. From this, a great amount of information can be gathered on key factors which might include:

- Award dollar amount

- Types of position

- Promotion method.

From this, many valuable improvements can be identified and implemented. What you might find is that there is a certain dollar amount, beyond which additional money doesn't really create additional benefits, and that additional money can be directed into the most optimal promotion methods rather than raising the award amount. Many organizations have broken away from the one-size-fits-all award amounts and are offering different amounts for certain types of positions, for instance, a $1,000 standard bonus and a $2,000 bonus for engineering or sales positions. Rather than basing this simply on need or value to the company for the positions (engineering or sales), an optimal solution can be created that is based on facts and not just guesses. In a large organization, the value of optimization can result in significant positive bottom-line results.

Remember: *Design of Experiments can be an invaluable tool in optimizing a process, but it should probably be used only after you have initial improvements already in place.* While any size organization can benefit from DOE, larger organizations have an opportunity to create significant improvements due to a larger body of data to draw on and the scalability of any optimization that is created.

A rule of thumb for Design of Experiments is that about 50% of your time and effort should be spent setting up the design to make sure it addresses the goals of the experiment.

Trial	Award Dollar Amount			Types of Positions			Promotion		Result
	$500	$1000	$2000	Engi-neering	Sales	Other Positions	Email	Contest	
1	x			x			x		
2		x		x			x		
3			x	x			x		
4	x				x		x		
5		x			x		x		
6			x		x		x		
7	x					x	x		
8		x				x	x		
9			x			x	x		
10	x			x				x	
11		x		x				x	
12			x	x				x	
13	x				x			x	
14		x			x			x	
15			x		x			x	
16	x					x		x	
17		x				x		x	
18			x			x		x	

FIGURE Appendix-1

Regression Analysis vs. Design of Experiments

If both tools look at multiple variables, what are the primary differences?

Regression analysis looks at past (historical) data and attempts to draw conclusions from it to predict future data and to identify what factors are most important.

Design of Experiments is just that: an experiment. It takes different factors and manipulates them in various combinations and records the outcomes to see which factors or combination of factors can drive outcomes in a desired way.

Failure Mode and Effects Analysis (FMEA)

Failure Mode and Effects Analysis (FMEA) is an exercise that allows us to isolate the possible things that can go wrong with a process and what these in turn might cause to happen. As we identify the possible things that could go wrong (failure modes), we can identify the reason (cause) and how that would impact the process (effect). We can then think about what might be done to cause them not to happen in the first place, or at least figure out how to mitigate the damage (control). We can utilize the FMEA exercise to identify these failure modes and also to prioritize them based on risk. We can score these failure modes by creating a score for each one's risk priority by looking at the following three things:

- Frequency (how often does the failure occur?)
- Severity (how much damage is done? How much of a problem is the failure mode to fix?)
- Customer Detection (is the customer likely to notice and care about this failure?)

By scoring each of these with a 1–10 score and then adding them up, you come up with a score that shows the risk of each failure.

Risk = Frequency + Severity + Customer Detection

Let's look at two simple examples from a benefit open enrollment process:

Benefit Open Enrollment			Score				
Failure Mode	**Cause**	**Effect**	Frequency	Severity	Customer Detection	**Total**	**Control**
Incorrect or no postage put on return envelope of benefit package	Error by employee	Packet returned and open enrollment deadline missed	2	8	10	20	Use prepaid envelopes
No signature on beneficiary forms	1) Error by employee 2) Signature line not clearly marked	Forms must be returned for signature and packets delayed	3	8	3	15	1) Mark signature page with highlighted color or other flag 2) Include reminder note on back of envelope to make sure forms are signed

FIGURE Appendix-2

Incorrect or no postage put on return envelope of benefit package: This failure may be caused by the employee simply forgetting to put stamps on the envelope or not putting the correct amount of postage on, which causes the post office to return the envelope to the sender. This doesn't happen often, so the frequency is scored as a 2. The severity is put at an 8, because it may cause the open enrollment deadline to be missed. The customer detection is scored as a 10 because the post office (another customer of the process) will almost always detect missing or incorrect postage and return the package to sender or deliver it with postage due to the recipient. This gives us a final score of 20. The simplest fix to this is to provide postage-paid envelopes that are billed to the company based on usage and weight.

No signature on beneficiary forms: If beneficiary forms are not signed by the employee, this can cause a delay in the process because the forms must be returned to the employee for signature and then resent to the benefits department. This happens infrequently, so it is scored a 3. The severity is scored as an 8 because it can delay the open enrollment process and cause deadlines to be missed. The customer (employee) is unlikely to detect this when they send in their packet, so it is scored with a 3. This gives us a final score of 15. The possible fixes to control the problem are to prominently mark the spots on the forms that require a signature and/or put an additional reminder on the back of the envelope that reminds the employee to sign the forms wherever it is necessary.

These are just simple examples of FMEA. The causes and effects could be much more detailed considering the many ways a process may have variation and how a failure might impact a process. This is meant to be an exhaustive process and some remote possible failure modes would be included in this exercise through brainstorming and the past experiences of the project team. By utilizing the three scores (frequency, severity, and customer detection), the possible failures can be prioritized to spend resources and energy first on those that are most likely to happen, cause the most damage, or be noticed by a customer.

Final Thought

This is just a brief sampling of additional ways to analyze data to improve your processes. Utilizing these tools effectively will take additional study and it may be recommended that you enlist outside help to mentor you on their proper use. This Appendix was designed to help you become more aware of these advanced tools and what the *next level* looks like as you get better and better at improving your HR operations and striving for excellence.

Additional information on advanced tools is available in the Online Resource Center.

GLOSSARY OF TERMS

Activity-Based Costing (ABC). Activity-Based Costing is a type of accounting that gauges the true costs of specific processes. It looks at the individual steps in a process and not just the overhead costs of a department or process.

Adaptability. Part of measuring the quality of a project, i.e., the ability to be both effective and efficient in the face of change, which will determine the sustainability of results over time and will be where the true return on investment will be realized.

Alignment. How well a project balances the goals and objectives of the business as well as the specific goals and priorities of the HR department.

Analysis of Variation (ANOVA). A statistical test of different sets of data to determine whether variation in measures has an impact on process outputs. ANOVA establishes a level of confidence in whether variations are tied to a particular factor, or can be explained by random chance or natural variation.

Availability of Resources. One of the key constraints that factors into project selection because there may not be enough time, staff, and/or budget.

Bar Charts. A useful tool comparing a measurement (or several measurements) from different items.

Benchmarking. An improvement process in which a company measures its performance against that of best-in-class companies, determines how those companies achieved their performance levels, and uses the information to improve its own performance. The subjects that can be benchmarked include strategies, operations, processes and procedures. (See p. 118.)

Breakthrough process improvement. A drastic improvement approach that abandons the existing process and creates a completely new process based on customer requirements.

Business Process Outsourcing (BPO). The leveraging of technology or specialist process vendors to provide and manage an organization's critical and/or non-critical enterprise processes and applications. The most common examples of BPO are call centers, human resources, accounting and payroll outsourcing.

Causal analysis. Identifying the causes, correlations, and interconnections of various processes.

Cause-and-Effect / Fishbone Diagram. A chart tool, usually in the shape of a fish, used to understand the root causes of different effects. (See Ishigawa Diagram.)

Change Management. Change management can take many forms and include many change environments. The most common usage of the term refers to organizational change management. Organizational change management is the process of developing a planned approach to change in an organization. Typically, the objective is to maximize the collective benefits for all people involved in the change and minimize the risk of failure of implementing the change. The discipline of change management deals primarily with the human aspect of change, and is therefore related to pure and industrial psychology.

Combine. Part of the E-S-C-A-P-E Method. It refers to combining tasks to simplify and eliminate tasks. This can mean integrating tasks that were previously done as separate steps, or adjusting the timing of when the steps are done. (See E-S-C-A-P-E Method.)

Compliance. Refers to systems or departments at corporations and public agencies to ensure that personnel are aware of, and take steps to comply with, relevant laws and regulations.

Control Charts. A statistical tool that analyzes data over time to spot trends and to ensure project completion.

Cost/Benefit. The relationship between the cost of the project and the measurable outcomes.

Critical To Quality Factors (CTQs). Key inputs in a process that have a definitive impact on the process outputs.

cross-functional map. Another form of process mapping that helps analyze how work is shared among different departments, people, and outside entities. This map is also often referred to as a swim lane map. (See Swim Lane Map.)

current state. A process map that shows what the current process looks like.

Customer Detection. Whether a customer will notice a defect or mistake in a service. (See Failure Mode and Effects Analysis.)

Customer Relationship Management (CRM). Encompasses the capabilities, methodologies, and technologies that support an enterprise in managing customer relationships. The general purpose of CRM is to enable organizations to better manage their customers through the introduction of reliable systems, processes, and procedures.

customer requirements. The broad elements of what internal and external customers need to execute their processes.

Customer Service. The provision of labor and other resources for the purpose of increasing the engagement value that internal and external customers receive from an organization.

Dashboard Metrics. Smaller grouping of metrics that represent key performance indicators of HR operations. These are broad measurements such as turnover, cost-per-hire, benefits expenditures per employee, etc. These may also be even higher level numbers (organizational scorecard numbers) which look at the overall performance of the organization.

Design of Experiments (DOE). A systematic but complex approach that analyzes many different variables (or factors) that play a part in the outcome of a process. While a small organization may also benefit from this approach, a large organization would be the most likely user.

desired state. A process map that shows what the process will ideally look like after improvements are made.

DMAIC. The basic structure of the general Six Sigma approach to project improvement. DMAIC (pronounced Di-MAY-ick) stands for Define, Measure, Analyze, Improve, and Control. (See Six Sigma.)

Effectiveness. Part of measuring the quality of a project, i.e., how well the process meets customer needs.

Efficiency. Part of measuring the quality of a project, i.e., the ability to be effective with the least amount of resources. This might be measured through cost-per-hire or recruiting efficiency metrics. The critical factor in this is the ability to be effective and to still meet customer needs while keeping costs under control.

Eliminate. Part of the E-S-C-A-P-E Method. It refers to what steps or tasks can be eliminated from a process. (See E-S-C-A-P-E Method.)

employee self-service (ESS). The use of online forms and automated workflow to empower employees and managers.

E-S-C-A-P-E Method. A process improvement approach that looks at tasks within a process and applies the following actions: Eliminate, Simplify, Combine, Automate, Parallel Path, and Empower.

Experience. Part of measuring the quality of a project, i.e., how being a part of the process feels for customer(s). An efficient, effective process that turns a blind eye to customer(s)' experience that may fall short (e.g., a poor experience for job applicants when applying online and having to spend unnecessary time with bureaucratic forms and procedures).

Failure Mode and Effects Analysis (FMEA). An analysis exercise that identifies the possible things that could go wrong (failure modes), the reasons (causes), and how the process would be impacted (effect).

Fishbone Diagram. See Cause-and-Effect/Fishbone Diagram.

Five "Whys." In root cause analysis, the process of asking why something functions the way it does, which can normally be accomplished in a series of five rounds or less.

Flowchart. Visual tool used to help identify the steps that take place in a process.

FMEA. See Failure Mode and Effects Analysis.

Force Field Analysis. A useful analysis technique for looking at the different forces that exist for and against a change. It is a graphical and analytical method of weighing pros and cons.

Frequency. Refers to how often a failure occurs in a Failure Mode and Effects Analysis. (See FMEA.)

Gap Analysis. An analysis tool that looks at the difference between (gap between) current process performance and customer requirements.

Gross Profit Margin. The profit margin shows how much profit a company makes for every $1 it generates in revenue. The Gross Profit Margin is the net sales minus the cost of goods and services sold.

Hard Dollars. Tangible monetary savings that is measurable and quantifiable.

Hawthorne Effect. A famous study of performance was conducted in Chicago from 1924 to 1933 at a factory named the Hawthorne Works of the Western Electric Company. This study was originally designed to understand the effect of how different levels of illumination would impact worker performance (i.e., whether brighter light or less light made productivity go up or down). The common takeaway of the experiment was that the performance of participants was changed more so by the fact that they knew they were being studied, rather than the actual factors being manipulated (illumination). This phenomenon was subsequently referred to as The Hawthorne Effect. (See p. 85.)

Histograms. A useful tool for breaking out process data into columns for determining frequencies of certain events or categories of data. These charts can help to show the most frequent causes of problems, distribution of process data, or provide other process-improvement information.

Human Resource Outsourcing (HRO). The leveraging of technology or specialist process vendors to provide and manage an organization's transactional and administrative human resources activities.

Incremental process improvement. An improvement approach that takes an existing process and tries to make adjustments to it while keeping the basic process intact.

Internal Service Level Agreement (SLA). A formal agreement between human resources and one of it's specific customers.

Ishigawa Diagram. A chart tool, usually in the shape of a fish, used to understand the root causes of different effects. Named after its creator, Kaoru Ishikawa, a Japanese consultant and leader in the scientific analysis of causes in industrial processes. (Also known as the Cause-and-Effect/ Fishbone Diagram.)

Lean Manufacturing. A management philosophy focusing on reduction of the seven wastes (Over-production, Waiting time, Transportation, Processing, Inventory, Motion, and Scrap) in manufactured products or any type of business.

manager self-service (MSS). The use of online forms and automated workflow to empower employees and managers.

methodologies. The collection, the comparative study, and the critique of the individual methods that are used in a given discipline or field of inquiry.

Mistake Proofing. Removing or putting controls in place to manage the factors that cause mistakes in a process.

Net Present Value (NPV). A standard method in finance of capital budgeting, i.e., the planning of long-term investments.

Net Profit Margin. The profit margin shows how much profit a company makes for every $1 it generates in revenue. The Net Profit Margin is the net income divided by net sales.

One Factor At a Time (OFAT). Looking at the individual parameters of a process, and trying to adjust one factor at a time in an effort to understand relationships to process outcomes.

Outsourcing. The delegation of non-core operations or jobs from internal production within a business to an external entity (such as a subcontractor or vendor) that specializes in that operation.

Pareto Analysis. (1) A histogram that is ranked with the column that has the highest frequency to the left and the column with the smallest frequency to the right. (See Histogram.) (2) The concept of the vital few, also known as the 80/20 rule, which was developed by an Italian mathematician named Pareto. The rule states that 80% of what happens is often influenced by 20% or less of the inputs.

Poke Yoke. See Mistake Proofing

Power User. A person empowered to learn the complexities of processes that are outside the reach of normal users, and then to pass on that information through tips and trainings.

Process Documentation. The act of identifying and recording processes.

Process Drawing. The physical illustration of a process by putting it down on paper, or by using a software program.

Process Improvement. The activity of elevating the performance of a process, especially that of a business process with regard to achieving its goal.

Process Mapping. The task of identifying and understanding the events that take place in a process.

Process Metrics. Metrics that represent the processes of HR operations. These are transactional measurements that may come from a check sheet or daily log, a spreadsheet, or other report, or a Human Resource Information System (HRIS).

Process Owner. The person responsible for a specific process like reviewing resumes.

Professional Employer Organization (PEO). A service provider utilizing a business relationship that allows outsourcing of human resources tasks, mainly for small to mid-sized businesses that do not have the need or resources for a dedicated human resources department.

Project Charter. A document that summarizes the key elements of a project.

Project Postmortem. A project postmortem analyzes what can be learned from the results of a completed project to improve on future projects.

Project Selection. Prioritizing and selecting which projects should be focused on first.

Qualitative. This is an indication of the positive and negative characteristics of the level of service, rather than simply the number of transactions in a process. (See Quantitative.)

Quality. A subjective term that can be simply defined in business as "meeting customer requirements."

Quantitative. This refers simply to the number of transactions in a process, rather than the positive and negative characteristics of the level of service. (See Qualitative.)

Regression Analysis. An analysis tool used to learn more about the relationship between several independent (predictor) variables and a dependent (criterion) variable. It takes historical data and creates a mathematical model that can be extrapolated and used to predict how the process will respond in the future.

Relationship Continuation Clause. A part of an outsourcing contract that allows the contract term to be extended to maintain "business-as-usual" while a new contract is being negotiated, or a transition is taking place to settle in a new vendor, or an operation is being brought back in-house.

Repeatable. Understanding if a method of measurement would glean the same result in each subsequent measurement.

Request for Information (RFI). A standard business process to collect written information about the capabilities of various suppliers. Normally, it follows a format that can be used for comparative purposes.

Request for Proposal (RFP). A standard business invitation for suppliers, through a bidding process, to bid on a specific product or service.

Return on Investment (ROI). A comparison of the money earned (or lost) on an investment to the amount of money invested.

Root Cause Analysis. The process of asking why something functions the way it does, which can normally be accomplished in a series of five rounds or less. (See Five "Whys.")

Run Chart. A statistical tool that analyzes data over time to spot trends and to ensure project completion.

Sampling. The part of statistical practice concerned with the selection of individual observations intended to yield some knowledge about a population of concern, especially for the purposes of statistical inference.

Scatter Plots. An analysis tool that reveals whether or not there is a correlation between two variables.

Scope Creep. Refers to uncontrolled changes in a project's scope. This phenomenon can occur when the scope of a project is not properly defined, documented, and controlled.

Service Level Agreement (SLA). A formal agreement between the supplier of a service and the user of that service (customer).

Service Level Management (SLM). The effort to manage the quality and quantity of services delivered.

Severity. Refers to how much of a problem the failure mode is to fix. (See FMEA.)

Shared Services. The convergence and streamlining of an organization's functions to ensure that they deliver the services required as effectively and efficiently as possible. This often involves the centralizing of back office functions such as HR and Finance, but can also be applied to the middle or front offices.

Simplify. Part of the E-S-C-A-P-E Method. It refers to reducing the amount of work needed to accomplish a task while still accomplishing the goal of the task. (See E-S-C-A-P-E Method.)

SIPOC. A graphical tool used to understand the key elements and phases of a process (pronounced Sigh-Pock). SIPOC stands for Supplier, Input, Process, Output, and Customer.

Six Sigma. A process-improvement methodology that was created by Motorola in the mid-1980s and made famous through its successful use by companies like General Electric in the mid- to late '90s. Six Sigma is a structured methodology that utilizes statistical analysis to improve processes. The basic structure of the general Six Sigma approach to project improvement is called DMAIC. (See DMAIC.)

SLA. See Service Level Agreement.

SLM. See Service Level Management.

Soft Dollars. Initially intangible elements that are difficult to measure and quantify. They often comprise a great deal of most process-improvement efforts: improved customer service, reduced stress from work, fewer mistakes that have to be corrected, and all of the other benefits that cascade into every area of an organization.

Stakeholders. Internal and external customers of an organization.

Standard Deviation. The square root of the variance, which measures how spread out the values in a data set are.

Strategy. A carefully devised plan of action to achieve a goal, or the art of developing or carrying out such a plan. (See Tactics.)

Success Probability. The likelihood of a project succeeding, which needs to be objectively looked at and considered, and must be weighed carefully in conjunction with a cost/benefit analysis. (See Cost-Benefit.)

Swim Lane Map. Another form of process mapping that helps analyze how work is shared among different departments, people, and outside entities. It is often referred to as a swim lane map because of the way it is set up to show rows that represent people or functions in the organization. These rows look similar to the lanes in a swimming pool. (See cross-functional map.)

Systems. An assemblage of processes comprising a whole, with each and every component/element interacting or related to another one.

Tactics. The set of actions taken to fulfill a strategy. (See Strategy.)

Total Cost of Ownership (TCO). A financial estimate designed to help organizations assess direct and indirect costs related to the purchase of any capital investment, such as (but not limited to) computer software or hardware.

Total Quality Management (TQM). A process-improvement methodology that focuses on eliminating waste, and which promotes continuous improvement.

Transition clauses. A legal clause in an outsourcing contract to ensure cooperation and support from the vendor during the ending of the contract and the transition to another vendor, or transfer back in-house to the customer organization.

Value. What is created and measured by dividing the worth by the cost of an activity.

Variation. Differences in the results of a process. Cycle time and quality are common factors that vary in a process.

Voice of the Customer (VOC). The process of engaging the stakeholders to find out what their needs are.

Waste. The inefficient use of resources in a process by expending time or money in a way that does not add value. This can include doing things that are not required by the customer, or having to do things over because of mistakes or poor quality.

BIBLIOGRAPHY
AND
REFERENCES

American Society for Quality (2002). Quality Glossary. *Quality Progress*, 35(7) pp. 43–61.

Aristotle, *Brainyquote.* <http://www.brainyquote.com/quotes/quotes/a/aristotle145967.html>

Becker, B. E., Huselid, M. A. & Ulrich, D. A. (2001) *The HR Scorecard: Linking People Strategy, and Performance.* Boston: Harvard University Press.

Bergdahl, Michael. *Brainyquote.* <http://www.brainyquote.com/quotes/quotes/m/michaelber227710.htm>

Blackburn, R., & Rosen, B. (1995). Does HRM Walk the TQM Talk? *HR Magazine*, 40(7), 69(3) Full text retrieved May 1, 2004 from EbscoHost database.

Bowen, D. E., & and Lawler, E. E., III (1992, Spring). "Total Quality-Oriented Human Resources Management," *Organizational Dynamics*, 20(4), p. 29–41.

Brassard, M. & Ritter, D. (2001) *Sailing through Six Sigma: How the Power of People Can Perfect Processes and Drive Down Costs.* Marietta, GA: Brassard & Ritter, LLC.

Bush, D. F., Danner, D. W., Morgenstern, G. & O'Connell, A. K. (1992). "Human Resource Involvement in Corporate Quality." Paper presented at the 1992 ASQC Quality Congress Transactions—Nashville. Paper retrieved January 28, 2005 from ASQ online member library http://www.asq.org.

Caudron, S. (1993). "How HR Drives TQM." *Personnel Journal*, 72(8), 48A–48O.

Chaudron, D. (1992). "HR and TQM: all aboard!" *HR Focus*, 69(11), pp. 1, 6.

Clinton, R. J., Williamson, S., & Bethke, A. L. (1994). "Implementing Total Quality Management: the Role of Human Resource Management." *SAM Advanced Management Journal*, 59(2), 10(7). Full text retrieved May 1, 2004 from EbscoHost database.

Coke, Edward, *Brainyquote*. < http://www.brainyquote.com/quotes/quotes/e/edwardcoke186743.html>

Cottrill, K. (2002, August 19). "Seeking Perfection: Process Improvement Methodology Works Even in Hard-To-Measure Service Organizations." *Traffic World*, 266(33), 13–14.

Defeo, J. A. (1999, July). "Six Sigma: Road Map for Survival." *HR Focus*, 76(7), 11–12. Full text retrieved May 1, 2004 from EbscoHost database.

Defeo, J. A. (2000a). "An ROI Story." *Training & Development*, 54, 25(3). Full text retrieved May 1, 2004 from EbscoHost database.

Defeo, J. A. (2000b). "Six Sigma: New Opportunities for HR, New Career Growth for Employees." *Employment Relations Today*, 27(2), p1(6). Full text retrieved May 1, 2004 from EbscoHost database.

Deming, W. Edwards. *Brainyquote*. <http://www.brainyquote.com/quotes/quotes/w/wedwardsd121224 html> <http://www.brainyquote.com/quotes/quotes/w/wedwardsd133510.html>

Deming, W. Edwards. (1986). *Out of the Crisis*. MIT Press, Cambridge, MA.

Dusharme, D. (2001). "Six Sigma Survey: Breaking through the Six Sigma Hype." *Quality Digest*, November http://www.qualitydigest.com/nov01/html/sixsigmaarticle.html.

Dusharme, D. (2003a February). "Six Sigma Survey: Big Success . . . but what about the other 98 percent?" *Quality Digest*, <http://www.qualitydigest.com/nov03/articles/01_article.shtml>

Dusharme, D. (2003b November). "Survey: Six Sigma Packs a Punch." *Quality Digest*. <http://www.qualitydigest.com/nov03/articles/01_article.shtml>

Dusharme, D. (2004). "Got Six Sigma on the Brain?" (2004 Six Sigma Survey) *Quality Digest*. Retrieved from http://www.qualitydigest.com/nov04/articles/01_article.shtml.

Eckes, G. (2001). *Making Six Sigma Last: Managing the Balance between Cultural and Technical Change*. New York: John Wiley and Sons, Inc.

Eckes, G. (2003a). *Six Sigma for Everyone*. New York: John Wiley and Sons, Inc.

Eckes, G. (2003b). *Six Sigma Team Dynamics: The Elusive Key to Project Success*. New York: John Wiley and Sons, Inc.

Fister Gale, S. (2003a, May). "Building Frameworks for Six Sigma Success." *Workforce*, 64–66.

Fister Gale, S. (2003b, May). *Six Sigma Is a Way of Life. Workforce*, 67–68.

Foulkes, M. & Keight, E. (2002). "Consumer-driven Six Sigma Applied to HR at Ford Motor Co." *Strategic HR Review*; 1(2), 26–30.

Frederico, M. & Thompson, T. (2003). "The Role of Human Resources (HR) in Six Sigma." *iSixSigma*. Retrieved on May 2, 2004 from: http://www. isixsigma.com/library/content/c030414a.asp?action=print.

Gallager, Robert C., *Brainyquotes*. <http://www.brainyquote.com/quotes/ quotes/r/robertcga104504.html>

Fitz-Ens, Jac. (1995, 1984) *How to Measure Human Resources Management*, Second Edition. McGraw Hill, New York.

George, M. L. (2002). *Lean Six Sigma: Combining Six Sigma Quality with Lean Speed*. New York: McGraw Hill.

George, M. L. (2003). *Lean Six Sigma for Service: How to Use Lean Speed & Six Sigma Quality to Improve Services and Transactions*. New York: McGraw Hill.

Goldwyn, Samuel. *Brainyquote*. <http://www.brainyquote.com/quotes/quotes/ s/samuelgold122394.html>

Greaver, Maurice. F. (1999) "Strategic Outsourcing: A Structured Approach to Outsourcing Decisions and Initiatives," AMACOM, New York, p. 9.

Hammonds, K. (2005). "Why We Hate HR." *Fast Company Magazine*, 97, August 2005, p. 40.

Hawthorn Effect, *Wikipedia*. <http://en.wikipedia.org/wiki/Hawthorne_effect>

Henry, Brad, *Brainyquote*. <http://www.brainyquote.com/quotes/quotes/b/ bradhenry167817.html>

"HR Outsourcing Continues to Boom as Organizations Gain Experience and Reap Benefits," (April 18, 2005). *Business Wire*.

Iacocca, Lee. *Brainyquote*. <http://www.brainyquote.com/quotes/quotes/l/ leeiacocca149248.html>

IOMA Human Resources Department Management Report. (2003). "How a Six Sigma Process in the HR Dept. Saved $350,000" at E3, 3(4), 1, 3, 6.

Ishigawa, Kaoru. *Wikipedia*. <http://en.wikipedia.org/wiki/Kaoru_Ishikawa>

Laabs, J. J. (1995). "Prudential Measures HR with a Total-Quality Yardstick,"- *Personnel Journal,* 74(4), Full text retrieved May 1, 2004 from EbscoHost database.

Lanyon, S. (2003). "At Raytheon Six Sigma Works, Too, To Improve HR Management Processes." *Journal of Organizational Excellence,* 22(4), 29–42.

Maslow, Abraham, *Brainyquote.* <http://www.brainyquote.com/quotes/quotes/a/abrahammas107087.html>

Quality (2002) "Quality Glossary." *Quality Progress,* 35(7) 43–61.

Rees, C. (1995). "Quality management and HRM in the Service Industry: Some Case Study Evidence." *Employee Relations,* 17(3), 99(11). Full text retrieved May 1, 2004 from EbscoHost database.

Robbins, Anthony. *Brainyquote.* <http://www.brainyquote.com/quotes/quotes/t/tonyrobbin130551.html>

Ryan, J. T. (1995). "Is Total Quality fading as a strategy?" *HR Focus,* 72(10), 14–15.

Scherkenbach, W. W. (1991). *Deming's Road to Continual Improvement.* SPC Press, Knoxville, TN.

Schonberger, R. J. (1994 Summer). "Human Resource Management Lessons from a Decade of Total Quality Management and Reengineering." *California Management Review,* 109–122.

Segalla, E. (1989). "All for Quality and Quality for All." *Training & Development Journal,* 43(9), 36(10). Full text retrieved May 1, 2004 from EbscoHost database.

Simmons, D. E., Shadur, M. A., & Preston, A. P. (1995) "Integrating TQM and HRM." *Employee Relations,* 17(3), 75(12). Full text retrieved May 1, 2004 from EbscoHost database.

Snape, E. & Wilkinson, A. (1995). "Managing Human Resources for TQM: Possibilities and Pitfalls." *Employee Relations,* 17(3), 42(10). Full text retrieved May 1, 2004 from EbscoHost database.

Soltani, E. (2003). "Towards a TQM-driven HR Performance Evaluation: An Empirical Study." *Employee Relations,* 25(4), 347.

Wyper, B. & Harrison, A. (2000). "Deployment of Six Sigma Methodology in Human Resource Function: A Case Study." *Total Quality Management,* 11 (4–6), 720–728.

Yang, H. (1998). "The Effects of HR Systems and the Interaction Effects between HR Practices and HR Systems on Firm Performance: A Longitudinal Study." *Human Resource Management.* University of Minnesota.

INDEX

Acknowledgments

I would like to thank Kevin Grossman for his guidance and expertise in all stages of the book. Kevin helped me plan this book, before the first words were even drafted, and I consider it to be as much his book as it is mine. Kevin is a friend, a colleague, and a mentor, and I am grateful to know him.

In addition, I would like to thank the other people who held prominent roles in helping me through their various contributions, including:

Howard Adamsky of HR Innovators for his thoughts as an industry leader and as someone who had been through this process before. His patience and time has been invaluable in this process. Howard's book, *Hiring and Retaining Top IT Professionals: The Guide for Savvy Hiring Managers and Job Hunters Alike* is also one I highly recommend.

Ricky Weisbroth for her editing acumen and for asking me tough questions and pointing out all the things that would make this a more valuable book for the reader.

Jayanta Acharyya at Catchcal, who took such pride in helping with illustrations and cheerfully suffered through the endless changes that took place as the book continued to evolve.

Desta Garrett, who helped guide me through the aesthetic aspects of publishing by adding her keen eye and sense of design in making things visually appealing and easier for the reader to navigate all the material that I wanted to cover.

Vicki Weiland, who gave the book its final polish and helped pull it all together with last minute suggestions to make the book even better.

I would also like to thank Kristine Whittler who acted as one of my primary lay-editors, and who gave the perspective of how a first-time HR person viewed the material. She helped bridge the gap between the different levels that this audience spanned and reminded me of when more context was necessary to avoid talking over the heads of some readers.

In addition, there are literally hundreds of other people, both in and out of the HR industry, who have contributed to this book. These include past clients, vendors, other industry evangelists, and all the people who have attended a seminar or speech, or read an article of mine, and who have taken the time to contact me with their feedback. Your questions, comments, and stories that you have shared have helped me understand the issues that needed to be addressed and the gaps in the HR body of knowledge that still needed to be completed.

Ultimately, you were all the impetus for this book and I hope I have served you well in bringing it to the HR community.

ABOUT THE AUTHOR

Photo by Kevyn Major Howard

SCOTT

WESTON

PhD, SPHR

A N industry expert on process improvement, outsourcing, and strategic alignment in HR, Scott is a consultant and frequent speaker and contributor to HR conferences and publications.

In addition to earning a BS, an MBA, and a PhD in Management, he holds prominent certifications in Quality Management, including a Six Sigma Black Belt through the American Society for Quality, and the Senior Professional in Human Resources (SPHR) designation through the Human Resources Certification Institute.